Learning CoreOS

Your one-stop guide for building, configuring, maintaining, and deploying one of the world's fastest growing OSes

Kingston Smiler. S

Shantanu Agrawal

BIRMINGHAM - MUMBAI

Learning CoreOS

First published: March 2016

Production reference: 1160316

Published by Packt Publishing Ltd.
Livery Place
35 Livery Street
Birmingham B3 2PB, UK.

ISBN 978-1-78588-830-4

www.packtpub.com

Credits

Authors
Kingston Smiler. S
Shantanu Agrawal

Reviewer
Aneesh Kumar

Acquisition Editor
Divya Poojari

Content Development Editor
Shali Deeraj

Technical Editor
Mohit Hassija

Copy Editors
Dipti Mankame
Jonathan Todd

Project Coordinator
Kinjal Bari

Proofreader
Safis Editing

Indexer
Priya Sane

Graphics
Kirk D'Penha

Production Coordinator
Shantanu N. Zagade

Cover Work
Shantanu N. Zagade

About the Authors

Kingston Smiler. S is a seasoned professional with 12 years of experience in software development and presales, encompassing wide range of skill set, roles, and industry verticals. He has solid expertise in data communication networking and software-based switching and routing solutions, and virtualization platforms such as OpenStack, OpenDaylight controller, Docker Containers, and CoreOS. He is currently working as an advisor and technical consultant for networking companies in the development of Layer2 and Layer3 IP protocols.

He also has working experience in building IoT sensor networks with IoT OSes such as RIOT and Contiki; SoCs such as Arduino, Raspberry Pi, and Intel Galileo; and IoT protocols such as 802.14.5 (Zigbee), 6lowpan, RPL, CoAP, and MQTT. He is interested in building small-scale robots using Arduino and ROS Robotics platforms.

Active in various networking standard bodies such as IETF, IEEE, and ONF, Kingston has proposed two drafts in TRILL WG and one draft in MPLS WG of IETF. With the current surge in SDN, virtualization, and NFV, his primary focus is towards these areas. He completed a bachelor of engineering degree in computer science from Madras University.

Kingston is also the author of *OpenFlow Cookbook, Packt Publishing*.

First and foremost, I would like to thank the lord to give me immense confidence and energy to start and complete this book successfully. I want to thank my kids, mother, brother, sister, and all my other family members for their support and encouragement. Thanks to my coauthor Shantanu Agrawal who helped me finish the book on time. Thanks to Shali and Divya for their reviews and helping me to finish this book despite their busy schedule. Special thanks to my wife for her patience and support in bringing up this book as most part of the book was written on weekends, at night, and during vacations.

Shantanu Agrawal has over 15 years of experience in the telecom industry working in systems having high transaction rates with scalable architectures. He has extensive experience of consulting for solutions, designing, and implementing high-performing and highly available software. He has exposure to the complete life cycle of the product development and deployment challenges. During his journey, he has worked on different hardware platforms and operating systems, such as proprietary UNIX-based hardware, embedded systems with real-time operating systems, Linux, Solaris, and so on. He has experience in the core network elements and protocols used in GSM/UMTS/LTE networks. He graduated from IIT BTU and did post-graduation from BITS Pilani.

I would thank my family for allowing me to squeeze their time for this book and for being understanding. I would also want to thank my coauthor Kingston Smiler for driving this to completion and for his excellent contributions.

About the Reviewer

Aneesh Kumar is a principal engineer and Cloud evangelist at Pramati Technologies. He is a developer, hacker, and DevOps. Aneesh brings with him over 7 years of in-depth experience in designing and building complex Cloud architecture and web platforms. He's passionate about open source technologies and cloud infrastructures at scale.

www.PacktPub.com

eBooks, discount offers, and more

Did you know that Packt offers eBook versions of every book published, with PDF and ePub files available? You can upgrade to the eBook version at www.PacktPub.com and as a print book customer, you are entitled to a discount on the eBook copy. Get in touch with us at customercare@packtpub.com for more details.

At www.PacktPub.com, you can also read a collection of free technical articles, sign up for a range of free newsletters and receive exclusive discounts and offers on Packt books and eBooks.

https://www2.packtpub.com/books/subscription/packtlib

Do you need instant solutions to your IT questions? PacktLib is Packt's online digital book library. Here, you can search, access, and read Packt's entire library of books.

Why subscribe?

- Fully searchable across every book published by Packt
- Copy and paste, print, and bookmark content
- On demand and accessible via a web browser

Table of Contents

Preface

As more and more applications are moving towards the cloud with server virtualization, there is a clear necessity to deploy the user applications and services very fast and make them reliable with assured SLA by deploying the services in a right set of servers. This becomes more complex when these services are dynamic in nature, which results in making these services autoprovisioned and autoscaled over a set of nodes. The orchestration of the user application is not limited to deploy the services in the right set of server or virtual machines rather to be extended to provide network connectivity across these services to provide **Infrastructure as a Service (IaaS)**. Compute, network, and storage are the three main resources to be managed by the cloud provider in order to provide (IaaS). Currently, there are various mechanisms to handle these requirements in more abstract fashion. There are multiple cloud orchestration frameworks, which can manage the compute, storage, and networking resources. OpenStack, Cloud Stack, and VMware vSphere are some of the cloud platforms that orchestrate these resource pools and provide IaaS.

The server virtualization provided by a Virtual Machine (VM) has its own overhead of running a separate instance of the operating system on every virtual machine. This brings down the number of VM instances that can be run on the server, which heavily impacts the operational expense. As Linux namespace, containers technologies, such as docker and rkt, are gaining its popularity; one more level of server virtualization can be introduced by deploying the application services inside a container rather than VM However, there is a necessity of an orchestration and clustering framework for the containers or dockers for deploying the services in the cluster, the discovery of the service and service parameters, providing network across these containers or dockers, and so on. CoreOS is developed for this purpose.

CoreOS is a light-weight cloud service orchestration operating system based on Google Chrome. CoreOS is developed primarily for orchestrating applications/services over a cluster of nodes. CoreOS extends the existing services provided by Linux to work for a distributed cluster and not limited to a single node.

What this book covers

Chapter 1, *CoreOS, Yet Another Linux Distro?*, explains the basics of containers, dockers, and high-level architecture of CoreOS.

Chapter 2, *Setting Up Your CoreOS Environment*, teaches you how to set up and run CoreOS with a single machine using Vagrant and VirtualBox. It also covers how to create and run docker images and get familiarized with the important configuration files and their contents.

Chapter 3, *Creating Your CoreOS Cluster and Managing the Cluster*, teaches you how to set up the CoreOS cluster with multiple machines. You will also learn how machines are discovered and services are scheduled on those machines. Also, you will learn about starting and stopping a service using Fleet.

Chapter 4, *Managing Services with User-Defined Constraints*, gives an introduction about service constraints, which helps to deploy services on suitable members.

Chapter 5, *Discovering Services Running in Cluster*, explains the need and mechanism for the discovery of services running on a cluster. Also, you will learn about two important tools, which are used widely for service discovery: etcdctl and curl.

Chapter 6, *Service Chaining and Networking Across Services*, explains the importance of the container communications and the various possibilities provided by CoreOS and docker to provide the communication.

Chapter 7, *Creating a Virtual Tenant Network and Service Chaining Using OVS*, explains the importance of OVS in container communications and the various advantages provided by OVS. The chapter details how the services deployed by different customers/tenants across the CoreOS cluster can be linked/connected using OVS.

Chapter 8, *What Next?*, touches upon some advanced Docker and Core OS topics and also discusses about what is coming up in CoreOS.

What you need for this book

The following software would be required for installing and bringing a sample CoreOS cluster.

- Git - https://git-scm.com/download
- VirtualBox - https://www.virtualbox.org/wiki/Downloads
- Vagrant - http://www.vagrantup.com/downloads

- VMware vSphere Client - `http://vsphereclient.vmware.com/vsphereclient/1/9/9/3/0/7/2/VMware-viclient-all-5.5.0-1993072.exe`

- CoreOS image for VMware - `http://stable.release.core-os.net/amd64-usr/current/coreos_production_vmware_ova.ova`

- Docker - `https://docs.docker.com/engine/installation/`

Who this book is for

This book is for cloud or enterprise administrators and application developers who would like to gain knowledge about CoreOS to deploy a cloud application or microservices on a cluster of cloud servers. It is also aimed at administrators with basic networking experience. You do not need to have any knowledge of CoreOS.

Conventions

In this book, you will find a number of text styles that distinguish between different kinds of information. Here are some examples of these styles and an explanation of their meaning.

Code words in text, database table names, folder names, filenames, file extensions, pathnames, dummy URLs, user input, and Twitter handles are shown as follows: "A directory, `coreos-vagrant`, is created after `git clone`."

A block of code is set as follows:

```
[Unit]
Description=Example
After=docker.service
Requires=docker.service

[Service]
TimeoutStartSec=0
ExecStartPre=-/usr/bin/docker kill busybox1
ExecStartPre=-/usr/bin/docker rm busybox1
ExecStartPre=/usr/bin/docker pull busybox
ExecStart=/usr/bin/docker run --name busybox1 busybox /bin/sh -c
"while true; do echo Hello World; sleep 1; done"
ExecStop=/usr/bin/docker stop busybox1
```

Any command-line input or output is written as follows:

```
weave status
...
          Service: dns
           Domain: weave.local.
         Upstream: 10.0.2.3
              TTL: 1
          Entries: 2

          Service: proxy
          Address: unix:///var/run/weave/weave.sock
```

New terms and **important words** are shown in bold. Words that you see on the screen, for example, in menus or dialog boxes, appear in the text like this: "Click on **Datastore ISO File** and select the uploaded iso file from the data store."

> Warnings or important notes appear in a box like this.

> Tips and tricks appear like this.

Reader feedback

Feedback from our readers is always welcome. Let us know what you think about this book—what you liked or disliked. Reader feedback is important for us as it helps us develop titles that you will really get the most out of.

To send us general feedback, simply e-mail feedback@packtpub.com, and mention the book's title in the subject of your message.

If there is a topic that you have expertise in and you are interested in either writing or contributing to a book, see our author guide at www.packtpub.com/authors.

Customer support

Now that you are the proud owner of a Packt book, we have a number of things to help you to get the most from your purchase.

Downloading the color images of this book

We also provide you with a PDF file that has color images of the screenshots/ diagrams used in this book. The color images will help you better understand the changes in the output. You can download this file from `https://www.packtpub.com/sites/default/files/downloads/LearningCoreOS_ColorImages.pdf`.

Errata

Although we have taken every care to ensure the accuracy of our content, mistakes do happen. If you find a mistake in one of our books—maybe a mistake in the text or the code—we would be grateful if you could report this to us. By doing so, you can save other readers from frustration and help us improve subsequent versions of this book. If you find any errata, please report them by visiting `http://www.packtpub.com/submit-errata`, selecting your book, clicking on the **Errata Submission Form** link, and entering the details of your errata. Once your errata are verified, your submission will be accepted and the errata will be uploaded to our website or added to any list of existing errata under the Errata section of that title.

To view the previously submitted errata, go to `https://www.packtpub.com/books/content/support` and enter the name of the book in the search field. The required information will appear under the **Errata** section.

Piracy

Piracy of copyrighted material on the Internet is an ongoing problem across all media. At Packt, we take the protection of our copyright and licenses very seriously. If you come across any illegal copies of our works in any form on the Internet, please provide us with the location address or website name immediately so that we can pursue a remedy.

Please contact us at `copyright@packtpub.com` with a link to the suspected pirated material.

We appreciate your help in protecting our authors and our ability to bring you valuable content.

Questions

If you have a problem with any aspect of this book, you can contact us at `questions@packtpub.com`, and we will do our best to address the problem.

1
CoreOS, Yet Another Linux Distro?

As more and more applications move toward the cloud with server virtualization, there is a clear necessity for deploying user applications and services very fast and reliably with assured SLA by deploying the services in the right set of servers. This becomes more complex when these services are dynamic in nature, which results in making these services auto-provisioned and auto-scaled over a set of nodes. The orchestration of the user application is not limited to deploying the services in the right set of servers or virtual machines, rather to be extended to provide network connectivity across these services to provide **Infrastructure as a Service (IaaS)**. Compute, network, and storage are the three main resources to be managed by the cloud provider in order to provide IaaS. Currently, there are various mechanisms to handle these requirements in a more abstract fashion. There are multiple cloud orchestration frameworks that can manage compute, storage, and networking resources. OpenStack, Cloud Stack, and VMware vSphere are some of the cloud platforms that perform orchestration of these resource pools and provide IaaS. For example, the Nova service in OpenStack manages the compute resource pool and creates VMs; the Neutron service provides the required information to provide virtual network connectivity across VMs; and so on.

The IaaS cloud providers should provide all three resources on-demand to the customers, which provide a pay-as-you-go model. The cloud provider maintains these resources as a pool and allocates the resource to a customer on-demand. This provides flexibility for the customer to start and stop the services based on their business needs and can save their OPEX. Typically, in an IaaS model, the cloud service provider offers these resources as a virtualized resource, that is, a virtual machine for compute, a virtual network for network, and virtual storage for storage. The hypervisor running in the physical server/compute nodes provides the required virtualization.

Typically, when an end user requests an IaaS offering with a specific OS, the cloud provider creates a new **VM (Virtual Machine)** with the OS requested by the user in their cloud server infrastructure. The end user can install their application in this VM. When the user requests more than one VM, the cloud provider should also provide the necessary network connectivity across these VMs in order to provide connectivity across the services running inside these VMs. The cloud orchestration framework takes care of instantiating the VMs in one of the available compute nodes in the cluster, along with associated services like providing virtual network connectivity across these VMs. Once the VM has been spawned, configuration management tools like Chef or Puppet can be used to deploy the application services over these VMs. Theoretically, this works very well.

There are three main problems with this approach:

- All the VMs in the system should run their own copy of the operating system with their own memory management and virtual device drivers. Any application or services deployed over these VMs will be managed by the OS running in the VM. When there are multiple VMs running in a server, all the VMs run a separate copy of OS, which results in overhead with respect to CPU and memory. Also, as the VMs run their own operating system, the time taken to boot/bring up a VM is very high.

- The operating system doesn't provide service-level virtualization that is running a service/application over a set of VMs which are part of cluster. The OS running in the VM is a general purpose operating system that lacks the concept of clustering and deploying the application or service over this cluster. In short, the operating system provides machine-level virtualization and not service-level virtualization.

- The management effort required to deploy a service/software from a development to a production environment is very high. This is because each software package typically has dependencies with other software. There are thousands of packages; each package comes with a different set of configuration, with most combinations of configurations having dependency with respect to performance and scaling.

CoreOS addresses all these problems. Before looking into how CoreOS solves these problems, we will look at a small introduction to CoreOS.

Introduction to CoreOS

CoreOS is a lightweight cloud service orchestration operating system based on Google's Chrome OS. CoreOS is developed primarily for orchestrating applications/ services over a cluster of nodes. Every node in the cluster runs CoreOS and one of the CoreOS nodes in the cluster will be elected as the master node by the etcd service. All the nodes in the cluster should have connectivity to the master node. All the slave nodes in the system provide information about the list of services running inside their system, along with the configuration parameter to the master node. In order to do this, we may have to configure fleet units in such a way that when we start a fleet unit with the `fleetctl` command, it should push its details such as IP and port to the etcd service. It is the responsibility of the master node to receive the service information and publish to all the other nodes in the cluster. In normal circumstances, the slave nodes won't talk to each other regarding service availability. The etcd service running in all the nodes in the cluster is responsible for electing the master node. All nodes in the system interact with the etcd service of the master node to get the service and configuration information of the services running in all other nodes. The following diagram depicts the CoreOS cluster architecture, wherein all the nodes in the cluster run CoreOS and other vital components of CoreOS like etcd, systemd, and so on. The etcd and fleet services are used for service discovery and cluster management respectively. In this, all three nodes are configured with the same cluster ID, so that all these nodes can be part of a single cluster. It is not possible for a node to be part of multiple clusters.

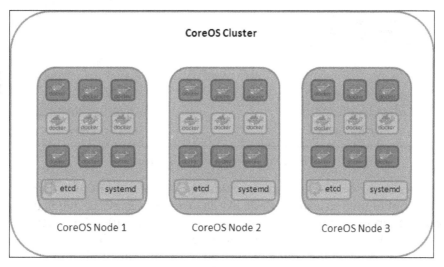

CoreOS cluster

All the applications or services are deployed as a Linux container in the CoreOS. The Linux container provides a lightweight server virtualization infrastructure without running its own operating system or any hypervisor. It uses the operating system-level virtualization techniques provided by the host OS using the namespace concept. This provides drastic improvements in terms of scaling and performance of virtualization instances running over the physical server. This addresses the first issue of running the application inside a VM.

The following diagram depicts the difference between applications running inside a VM and applications running in an LXC container. In the following diagram, the VM way of virtualization has a guest OS installed in the VM along with the host OS. In a Linux container-based implementation, the container doesn't have a separate copy of the operating system; rather, it uses the service provided by the host operating system for all the OS-related functionalities.

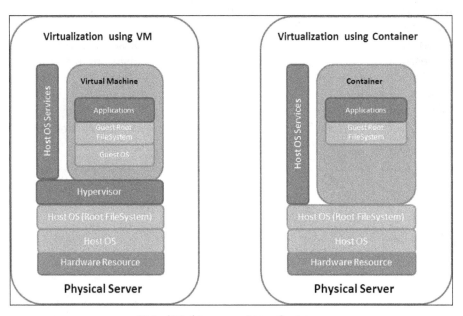

Virtual Machine versus Linux Container

CoreOS extends the existing services provided by Linux to work for a distributed cluster and not limited to a single node. As an example, CoreOS extends the system management service provided by most of the Linux distribution for starting, stopping, or restarting any applications/services to run on a cluster of nodes rather than a single node using the fleet tool. Instead of running an application limited to its own node, the services are submitted to fleet, which acts as a cluster manager and instantiates the service in any one of the nodes in the cluster. It is also possible to launch the container in a specific set of nodes by applying a constraint. This addresses the second issue with using VMs, discussed earlier in this chapter.

CoreOS uses Docker/Rocket as a container to deploy services inside the CoreOS cluster. Docker provides an easy way of bundling a service and its dependent module as a single monolithic image that can be shipped from development. In the deployment, the DevOps person can simply fetch the docker container from the development person and can deploy directly into the CoreOS nodes without performing any operations like building a compilation or build environment and rebuilding the image on the target platform and so on. This bridges the gap between the development and deployment of a service. This addresses the third issue with using VM, discussed earlier in this chapter.

CoreOS versus other Linux distributions

Even though CoreOS is yet another Linux distribution like Fedora/Centos, the key difference between CoreOS and other standard Linux distributions are as follows:

- CoreOS is not designed to run any applications or services directly. Any application to be run inside CoreOS should be deployed as a container (which can either be Docker/Rocket). So it is not possible to install any software packages in CoreOS and hence CoreOS doesn't have any installation software packages like `yum`, `apt`, and so on. In short, CoreOS is a stripped-down version of a Linux distribution that doesn't have any inbuilt user applications or library installed.

- Most of the Linux distributions are meant to run as a host operating system either in a data center server or in a typical desktop PC. They are not developed to manage a cluster of nodes/the cloud; rather, they will be part of the cloud that is being managed by other cloud orchestration platforms. However, CoreOS is a Linux distribution that is builtout for the management of a massive server infrastructure with clustering. The CoreOS cluster is a group of physical or virtual machines that runs CoreOS with the same cluster ID. The services running in the cluster nodes are managed by fleet, which is the CoreOS orchestration tool. Software updates in a traditional Linux distribution are done by updating the packages one by one. However, CoreOS supports a scheme called **fast patch**, wherein the entire CoreOS OS is updated once. The **CoreUpdate** program is used for updating CoreOS in a server, cluster, or complete data center.

- CoreOS is extremely lightweight when compared to traditional Linux distributions.

CoreOS high-level architecture

The CoreOS node in a cluster comprises the following main components:

- etcd
- systemd
- fleet
- Docker/Rocket containers

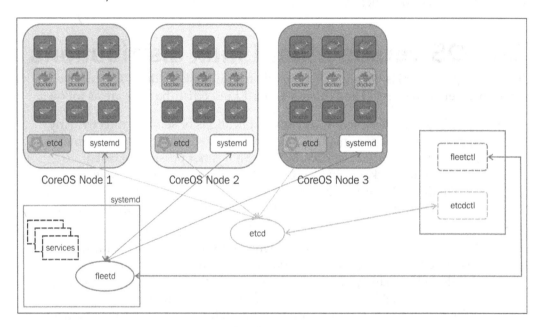

CoreOS High-level Architecture

The CoreOS node runs etcd, systemd, and the fleet service in all of the nodes in the cluster. etcd, which is running in all the nodes, talk to each other and elects one node as the master node. All the services running inside the node will be advertised to this master node, which makes etcd provide a service discovery mechanism. Similarly, fleetd running in different nodes maintains the list of services running in different nodes in its service pool, which provides service-level orchestration. `fleetctl` and `etcdctl` are command-line utilities to configure the fleet and etcd utilities respectively.

Refer to subsequent sections of this chapter to understand the functionality of each component in detail.

These components together provide three main functionalities for CoreOS as follows:

- Service discovery
- Cluster management
- Container management

Service discovery

In the CoreOS environment, all user applications are deployed as services inside a container that can either be a Docker container or a Rocket container. As different applications/services are running as separate containers in the CoreOS cluster, it is inevitable to announce the services provided by each node to all the nodes in the cluster. Along with service availability, it is also required that each service advertises the configuration parameters to other services. This service advertisement is very important when the services are tightly coupled and dependent on each other. For example, the web service should know details about the database services, about the connection string, or type of database and so on. CoreOS provides a way for each service to advertise its service and configuration information using the etcd service. The data announced to the etcd service will be given/announced to all the nodes in the cluster by the master node.

etcd

etcd is a distributed key value store that stores data across the CoreOS cluster. The etcd service is used for publishing services running on a node to all the other nodes in the cluster, so that all the services inside the cluster discover other services and configuration details of other services. etcd is responsible for electing the master node among the set of nodes in the cluster. All nodes in the cluster publish their services and configuration information to the etcd service of the master node, which provides this information to all the other nodes in the cluster.

Container management

The key element of the CoreOS building block is a container that can either be Docker or Rocket. The initial version of CoreOS officially supports Docker as the means for running any service application in the CoreOS cluster. In the recent version, CoreOS supports a new container mechanism called Rocket, even though CoreOS maintains backward compatibility with Docker support. All customer applications/services will be deployed as a container in the CoreOS cluster. When multiple services are running inside a server for different customers, it is inevitable to isolate the execution environment from one customer to another customer. Typically, in a VM-based environment, each customer will be given a VM and inside this VM the customer can run their own service, which provides complete isolation of the execution environment between customers. The container also provides a lightweight virtualization environment without running a separate copy of the VM.

Linux Container

Linux Container (LXC) is a lightweight virtualization environment provided by the Linux kernel to provide system-level virtualization without running a hypervisor. LXC provides multiple virtualized environments, each of them being inaccessible and invisible from the other. Thus, an application that is running inside one Linux container will not have access to the other containers.

LXC combines three main concepts for resource isolation as follows:

- Cgroups
- Namespaces
- Chroot

The following diagram explains in detail about LXC and the utilities required to provide LXC support:

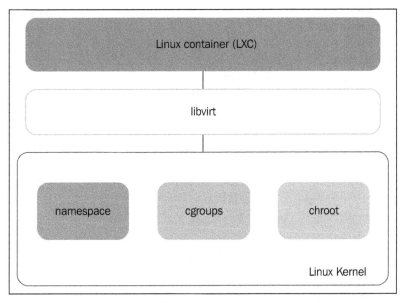

Linux Containers

Libvirt is a 'C' library toolkit that is used to interact with the virtualization capabilities provided by the Linux kernel. It acts as a wrapper layer for accessing the APIs exposed by the virtualization layer of the kernel.

cgroups

Linux **cgroups** is a feature provided by the kernel to restrict access to system resource for a process or set of processes. The Linux cgroup provides a way to reserve or allocate resources, such as CPU, system memory, network bandwidth and so on, to a group of processes/tasks. The administrator can create a cgroup and set the access levels for these resources and bind one or more processes to these groups. This provides fine-grained control over the resources in the system to different processes. This is explained in detail in the next diagram. The resources mentioned on the left-hand side are grouped into two different cgroups called cgroups-1 and cgroups-2. task1 and task2 are assigned to cgroups-1, which makes only the resources allocated for cgroups-1 available for task1 and task2.

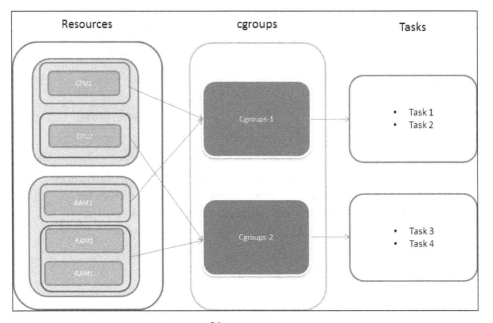

Linux cgroups

Managing cgroups consists of the following steps:

1. Creation of cgroups.
2. Assign resource limit to the cgroup based on the problem statement. For example, if the administrator wants to restrict an application not to consume more that 50 percent of CPU, then he can set the limit accordingly.
3. Add the process into the group.

As the creation of cgroups and allocation of resources happens outside of the application context, the application that is part of the cgroup will not be aware of cgroups and the level of resource allocated to that cgroup.

Namespace

namespace is a new feature introduced from Linux kernel version 2.6.23 to provide resource abstraction for a set of processes. A process in a namespace will have visibility only to the resources and processes that are part of that namespace alone. There are six different types of namespace abstraction supported in Linux as follows:

- PID/Process Namespace
- Network Namespace
- Mount Namespace
- IPC Namespace
- User Namespace
- UTS Namespace

Process Namespace provides a way of isolating the process from one execution environment to another execution environment. The processes that are part of one namespace won't have visibility to the processes that are part of other namespaces. Typically, in a Linux OS, all the processes are maintained in a tree with a child-parent relationship. The root of this process tree starts with a specialized process called init process whose process-id is 1. The init process is the first process to be created in the system and all the process that are created subsequently will be part of the child nodes of the process tree. The process namespace introduces multiple process trees, one for each namespace, which provides complete isolation of the processes running across different namespaces. This also brings the concept of a single process to have two different pids: one is the global context and other in the namespace context. This is explained in detail in the following diagram.

In the following diagram, for namespace, all processes have two process IDs: one in the namespace context and the other in the global process tree.

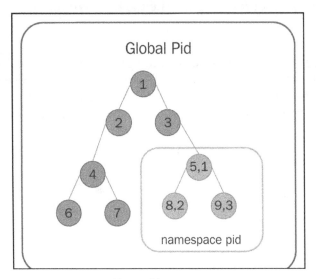

Process Namespace

Network Namespace provides isolation of the networking stack provided by the operating system for each container. Isolating the network stack for each namespace provides a way to run multiple same services, say a web server for different customers or a container. In the next diagram, the physical interface that is connected to the hypervisor is the actual physical interface present in the system. Each container will be provided with a virtual interface that is connected to the hypervisor bridging process. This hypervisor bridging process provides inter-container connectivity across the container, which provides a way for an application running in one container to talk to another application running in another container.

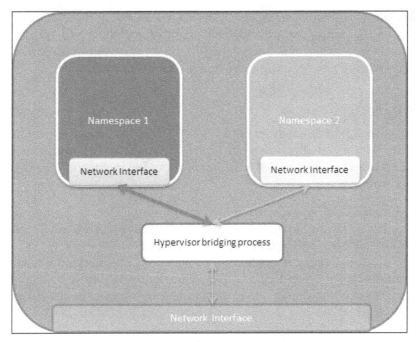

Network Namespace

Chroot

Chroot is an operation supported by Linux OS to change the root directory of the current running process, which apparently changes the root directory of its child. The application that changes the root directory will not have access to the root directory of other applications. Chroot is also called **chroot jail**.

Combining the cgroups, namespace, and chroot features of the Linux kernel provides a sophisticated virtualized resource isolation framework with clear segregation of the data and resources across various processes in the system.

In LXC, the chroot utility is used to separate the filesystem, and each filesystem will be assigned to a container that provides each container with its own root filesystem. Each process in a container will be assigned to the same cgroup with each cgroup having its own resources providing resource isolation for a container.

Docker

Docker provides a portable way to deploy a service in any Linux distribution by creating a single object that contains the service. Along with the service, all the dependent services can be bundled together and can be deployed in any Linux-based servers or virtual machine.

Docker is similar to LXC in most aspects. Similar to LXC, Docker is a lightweight server virtualization infrastructure that runs an application process in isolation, with resource isolation, such as CPU, memory, block I/O, network, and so on. But along with isolation, Docker provides *"Build, Ship and Run"* modeling, wherein any application and its dependencies can be built, shipped, and run as a separate virtualized process running in a namespace isolation provided by the Linux operating system.

Dockers can be integrated with any of the following cloud platforms: Amazon Web Services, Google Cloud Platform, IBM Bluemix, Jelastic, Jenkins, Microsoft Azure, OpenStack Nova, OpenSVC, and configuration tools such as Ansible, CFEngine, Chef, Puppet, Salt, and Vagrant. The following are the main features provided by Docker.

The main objective of Docker is to support micro-service architecture. In micro-service architecture, a monolithic application will be divided into multiple small services or applications (called micro-services), which can be deployed independently on a separate host. Each micro-service should be designed to perform specific business logic. There should be a clear boundary between the micro-services in terms of operations, but each micro-service may need to expose APIs to different micro-services similar to the service discovery mechanism described earlier. The main advantage of micro-service is quick development and deployment, ease of debugging, and parallelism in the development for different components in the system. One of the main advantage of micro-services is based on the complexity, bottleneck, processing capability, and scalability requirement; every micro-service can be individually scaled.

Docker versus LXC

Docker is designed for deploying applications, whereas LXC is designed to deploy a machine. LXC containers are treated as a machine, wherein any applications can be deployed and run inside the container. Docker is designed to run a specific service or application to provide container as an application. However, when an application or service has a dependency with other services, these services can also be packed along with the same Docker image. Typically, the docker container doesn't provide all the services that will be provided by any OS, such as init systems, syslog, cron, and so on. As Docker is more focused on deploying applications, it provides tools to create a docker container and deploy the services using source code.

Docker containers are designed to have a layered architecture with each layer containing changes from the previous version. The layered architecture provides the docker to maintain the version of the complete container. Like any typical version control tools like Git/CVS, docker containers are maintained with a different version with operations like commit, rollback, version tracking, version diff, and so on. Any changes made inside the docker application will be made as a read-only layer until it is committed.

Docker-hub contains more than 14,000 containers available for various well-known services that can be downloaded and deployed very easily.

Docker provides an efficient mechanism for chaining different docker containers, which provides a good service chaining mechanism. Different docker containers can be connected to each other via different mechanisms as follows:

- Docker link
- Using docker0 bridge
- Using the docker container to use the host network stack

Each mechanism has its own benefits. Refer to *Chapter 7, Creating a Virtual Tenant Network and Service Chaining Using OVS* for more information about service chaining.

Docker uses libcontainer, which accesses the kernel's container calls directly rather than creating an LXC.

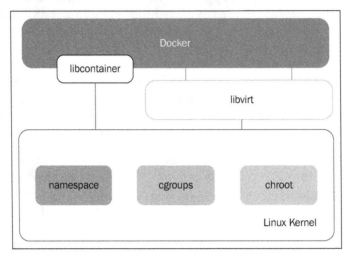

Docker versus LXC

Rocket

Historically, the main objective of CoreOS is to run the services as a lightweight container. Docker's principle was aligning with the CoreOS service requirement with simple and composable units as container. Later on, Docker adds more and more features to make the Docker container provide more functionality than standard containers inside a monolithic binary. These functionalities include building overlay networks, tools for launching cloud servers with clustering, building images, running and uploading images, and so on. This makes Docker more like a platform rather than a simple container.

With the previously mentioned scenario, CoreOS started working on a new alternative to Docker with the following objectives:

- Security
- Composability
- Speed
- Image distribution

CoreOS announced the development of Rocket as an alternative to Docker to meet the previously mentioned requirements. Along with the development of Rocket, CoreOS also started working on an App Container Specification. The specification explains the features of the container such as image format, runtime environment, container discovery mechanism, and so on. CoreOS launched its first version of Rocket along with the App Container Specification in December 2014.

CoreOS cluster management:

Clustering is the concept of grouping a set of machines to a single logical system (called cluster) so that the application can be deployed in any one machine in the cluster. In CoreOS, clustering is one of the main features provided by CoreOS by running different services/docker container over the cluster of the machine. Historically, in most of the Linux distribution, services can be managed using the systemd utility. CoreOS extends the systemd service from a single node to a cluster using fleet utility. The main reason for CoreOS to choose fleet to orchestrate the services across the CoreOS cluster is as follows:

- Performance
- Journal support
- Rich syntax in deploying the services

It is also possible to have a CoreOS cluster with a combination of a physical server and virtual machines as long as all the nodes in the cluster are connected to each other and reachable. All the nodes that want to participate in the CoreOS cluster should run CoreOS with the same cluster ID.

systemd

systemd is an init system utility that is used to stop, start, and restart any of the Linux services or user programs. systemd has two main terminologies or concepts: unit and target. **unit** is a file that contains the configuration of the services to be started, and **target** is a grouping mechanism to group multiple services to be started at the same time.

fleet

fleet emulates all the nodes in the cluster to be part of a single init system or system service. fleet controls the systemd service at the cluster level, not in the individual node level, which allows fleet to manage services in any of the nodes in the cluster. fleet not only instantiates the service inside a cluster but also manages how the services are to be moved from one node to another when there is a node failure in the cluster. Thus, fleet guarantees that the service is running in any one of the nodes in the cluster. fleet can also take care of restricting the services to be deployed in a particular node or set of nodes in a cluster. For example, if there are ten nodes in a cluster and among the ten nodes a particular service, say a web server, is to be deployed over a set of three servers, then this restriction can be enforced when fleet instantiates a service over the cluster. These restrictions can be imposed by providing some information about how these jobs are to be distributed across the cluster. fleet has two main terminologies or concepts: engine and agents. For more information about systemd and fleet, refer to chapter Creating Your CoreOS Cluster and Managing the Cluster.

CoreOS and OpenStack

Is CoreOS yet another orchestration framework like OpenStack/CloudStack? No, it is not. CoreOS is not a standalone orchestration framework like OpenStack/CloudStack. In most server orchestration frameworks, the framework sits external to the managed cloud. But in CoreOS, the orchestration framework sits along with the existing business solution.

OpenStack is one of the most widely used cloud computing software platforms to provide IaaS. OpenStack is used for orchestrating the compute, storage, and network entities of the cloud, whereas CoreOS is used for service orchestration. Once the compute, storage, or network entities are instantiated, OpenStack doesn't have any role in instantiating services inside these VMs.

Combining the orchestration provided by OpenStack and CoreOS provides a powerful IaaS, wherein the cloud provider will have fine-grained control until the service orchestration. So CoreOS can co-exist with OpenStack, wherein OpenStack can instantiate a set of VMs that run the CoreOS instance and form a CoreOS cluster. That is, OpenStack can be used to create a CoreOS cluster as infrastructure. The CoreOS that is running inside the VM forms as a cluster and instantiates the service inside any one of the nodes in the cluster.

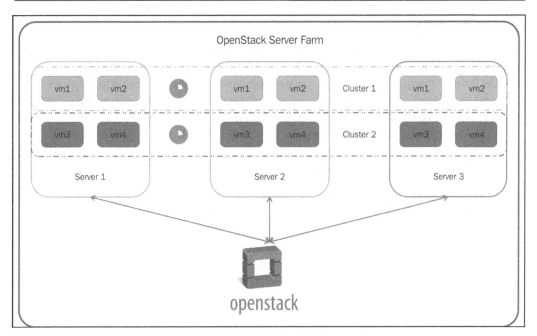

OpenStack and CoreOS

In the preceding diagram, OpenStack is used to manage the server farm that consists of three servers: server1, server2, and server3. When a customer is requested for a set of VMs, OpenStack creates the necessary VM in any one of these servers, as an IaaS offering. With CoreOS, all these VMs run the CoreOS image with the same cluster ID, and hence can be part of the same cluster. In the preceding diagram, there are two CoreOS clusters, each allocated for different customers. The services/applications to be run on these VMs will be instantiated by the fleet service of CoreOS, which takes care of instantiating the service in any one of the VMs in the cluster. At any point in time, OpenStack can instantiate new VMs inside the cluster in order to scale up the cluster capacity by adding new VMs running the CoreOS image with the same cluster ID, which will be a candidate for CoreOS to run new services.

Summary

CoreOS and Docker open up a new era for deploying the services in a cluster to streamline easy development and deployment of applications. CoreOS and Docker bridge the gap between the process of developing a service and deploying the service in production and make the server and service deployment less effort and less intensive work. With lightweight containers, CoreOS provides very good performance and provides an easy way to auto-scale the application with less overhead from the operator side. In this chapter, we have seen the basics of containers, Docker, and the high-level architecture of CoreOS.

In the next few chapters, we are going to see the individual building blocks of CoreOS in detail.

2
Setting Up Your CoreOS Environment

CoreOS can be installed on a variety of platforms such as bare metal servers, cloud provider's virtual machines, physical servers, and so on. This chapter describes in detail how to bring up your first CoreOS environment focusing on deploying CoreOS on a Virtual Machine. When deploying in a virtualization environment, tools such as Vagrant come in very handy in managing CoreOS virtual machines. **Vagrant** enables setting up CoreOS with multiple nodes even on single laptops or workstations easily with minimum configuration. Vagrant supports VirtualBox, a commonly used virtualization application. Both Vagrant and VirtualBox are available for multiple architecture, such as Intel or AMD, and operating systems such as Windows, Linux, Solaris, and Mac.

This chapter covers setting up CoreOS on VirtualBox, VMware VSphere, and the following topics:

- VirtualBox installation
- Introduction to Vagrant
- CoreOS on VMware VSphere setup
- Introduction to Docker

 GIT is used for downloading all the required software mentioned in this chapter.

Installing GIT

Download the latest version of GIT installation as per the host operating system from `https://git-scm.com/download`. After the download is complete, start the installation. The installation of GIT using this procedure is useful for Mac and Windows. For all Linux distributions, the GIT client is available through its package manager. For example, if the operation system is CentOS, the package manager `yum` can be used to install GIT.

Installing VirtualBox

Download the latest version of VirtualBox as per the host operating system and architecture from `https://www.virtualbox.org/wiki/Downloads`. After the download is complete, start the installation.

During installation, continue with the default options. VirtualBox installation resets the host machine's network adapters during installation. This will result in the network connection toggle. After the installation is successful, Installer will print the status of the operation.

Introduction to Vagrant

Vagrant provides a mechanism to install and configure a development, test, or production environment. Vagrant works with various virtualization applications such as VirtualBox, VMware, AWS and so on. All installation, setup information, configuration, and dependencies are maintained in a file and virtual machine can be configured and brought up using a simple Vagrant command. This also helps to automate the process of installation and configuration of machines using commonly available scripting languages. Vagrant helps in creating an environment that is exactly the same across users and deployments. Vagrant also provides simple commands to manage the virtual machines. In the context of CoreOS, Vagrant will help to create multiple machines of the CoreOS cluster with ease and with the same environment.

Installing Vagrant

Download and install the latest version of Vagrant from `http://www.vagrantup.com/downloads`. Choose default settings during installation.

Vagrant configuration files

The Vagrant configuration file contains the configuration and provisioning information of the virtual machines. The configuration filename is `Vagrantfile` and the file syntax is `Ruby`. The configuration file can be present in any of the directory levels starting from the current working directory. The file in the current working directory is read first, then the file (if present) in one directory level back, and so on until /. Files are merged as they are read. For most of the configuration parameters, newer settings overwrite the older settings except for a few parameters where they are appended.

A `Vagrantfile` template and other associated files can be *cloned* from the GIT repository (`https://github.com/coreos/coreos-vagrant.git`). Run the following command from the terminal to clone the repository. Note that the procedure to start a terminal may vary from OS to OS. For example, in Windows, the terminal for running GIT commands is by running `Git Bash`:

```
$ git clone https://github.com/coreos/coreos-vagrant/
```

A directory, `coreos-vagrant`, is created after `git clone`. Along with other files associated to the `Git` repository, the directory contains `Vagrantfile`, `user-data.sample`, and `config.rb.sample`. Rename `user-data.sample` to `user-data` and `config.rb.sample` to `config.rb`:

```
git clone https://github.com/coreos/coreos-vagrant/
Cloning into 'coreos-vagrant'...
remote: Counting objects: 402, done.
remote: Total 402 (delta 0), reused 0 (delta 0), pack-reused 402
Receiving objects: 100% (402/402), 96.63 KiB | 31.00 KiB/s, done.
Resolving deltas: 100% (175/175), done.

cd coreos-vagrant/
ls
config.rb.sample*  CONTRIBUTING.md*  DCO*  LICENSE*  MAINTAINERS*
NOTICE*  README.md*  user-data.sample*  Vagrantfile*
```

Vagrantfile contains template configuration to create and configure the CoreOS virtual machine using VirtualBox. Vagrantfile includes the config.rb file using the require directive:

```
...

CONFIG = File.join(File.dirname(__FILE__), "config.rb")
....

if File.exist?(CONFIG)
  require CONFIG
end

...


...

CLOUD_CONFIG_PATH = File.join(File.dirname(__FILE__), "user-data")
...

    if File.exist?(CLOUD_CONFIG_PATH)
      config.vm.provision :file, :source => "#{CLOUD_CONFIG_PATH}",
      :destination => "/tmp/vagrantfile-user-data"
      config.vm.provision :shell, :inline => "mv /tmp/vagrantfile-
      user-data /var/lib/coreos-vagrant/", :privileged => true
    end

...
```

Cloud-config

cloud config files are special files that get executed by the cloud-init process when the CoreOS system starts or when the configuration is dynamically updated. Typically, the cloud config file contains the various OS level configuration of the docker container such as networking, user administration, systemd units and so on. For CoreOS, user-data is the name of the cloud-config file and is present inside the base directory of the vagrant folder. The systemd units files are configuration files containing information about a process.

The cloud-config file uses the YAML file format. A cloud-config file must contain #cloud-config as the first line, followed by an associative array that has zero or more of the following keys:

- coreos: This key provides configuration of the services provided by CoreOS. Configuration for some of the important services are described next:

○ etc2: This key replaces the previously used `etc` service. The parameters for `etc2` are used to generate the systemd unit drop-in file for `etcd2` services. Some of the important parameters of the `etc2` configuration are:

`discovery`: This specifies the unique token used to identify all the etcd members forming a cluster. The unique token can be generated by accessing the free discovery service (`https://discovery.etcd.io/new?size=<clustersize>`). This is used when the discovery mechanism is used to identify cluster etcd members in cases where IP addresses of all the nodes are not known beforehand. The token generated is also called the discovery URL. The discovery service helps clusters to connect to each other using `initial-advertise-peer-urls` provided by each member by storing the connected etcd members, the size of the cluster, and other metadata against the discovery URL. For more information regarding forming the CoreOS cluster, refer to *Chapter 3, Creating Your CoreOS Cluster and Managing the Cluster.*

`initial-advertise-peer-urls`: This specifies the member's own peer URLs that are advertised to the cluster. The IP should be accessible to all etcd members. Depending on accessibility, a public and/or private IP can be used.

`advertise-client-urls`: This specifies the member's own client URLs that are advertised to the cluster. The IP should be accessible to all etcd members. Depending on accessibility, a public and/or private IP can be used.

`listen-client-urls`: This specifies the list of self URLs on which the member is listening for client traffic. All advertised client URLs should be part of this configuration.

`listen-peer-urls`: This specifies the list of self URLs on which the member is listening for peer traffic. All advertised peer URLs should be part of this configuration.

On some platforms, the providing IP can be automated by using *templating feature*. Instead of providing actual IP addresses, the fields `$public_ipv4` or `$private_ipv4` can be provided.

`$public_ipv4` is a substitution variable for the public IPV4 address of the machine.

`$private_ipv4` is a substitution variable for the private IPV4 address of the machine.

The following is sample `coreos` configuration in the `cloud-config` file:

```
#cloud-config
coreos:
  etcd2:
    discovery: https://discovery.etcd.io/d54166dee3e709cf35b
0d78913621df6
    # multi-region and multi-cloud deployments need to use
    $public_ipv4
    advertise-client-urls: http://$public_ipv4:2379
    initial-advertise-peer-urls: http://$private_ipv4:2380
    # listen on both the official ports and the legacy ports
    # legacy ports can be omitted if your application
doesn't
    depend on them
    listen-client-urls:
    http://0.0.0.0:2379,http://0.0.0.0:4001
    listen-peer-urls:
    http://$private_ipv4:2380,http://$private_ipv4:7001
```

- `fleet`: The parameters for fleet are used to generate environment variables for the fleet service. The fleet service manages the running of containers on clusters. Some of the important parameters of the fleet configuration are:

  `etcd_servers`: This provides the list of URLs through which etcd services can be reached. The URLs configured should be one of the `listen-client-urls` for etcd services.

  `public_ip`: The IP address that should be published with the local machine's state.

  The following is a sample fleet configuration in the `cloud-config` file:

```
#cloud-config
  fleet:
    etcd_servers: http:// $public_ipv4:2379,http:// $public_
ipv4:4001
    public-ip: $public_ipv4
```

- `flannel`: The parameters for flannel are used to generate environment variables for the flannel service. The flannel service provides communication between containers.

- ° locksmith: The parameters for locksmith are used to generate environment variables for the locksmith service. The locksmith service provides reboot management of clusters.

- ° update: These parameters manipulate settings related to how CoreOS instances are updated.

- ° Units: These parameters specify the set of systemd units that need to be started after boot-up. Some of the important parameters of unit configuration are:

name: This specifies the name of the service.

command: This parameter specifies the command to execute on the unit: start, stop, reload, restart, try-restart, reload-or-restart, reload-or-try-restart.

enable: This flag (true/false) specifies if the Install section of the unit file has to be ignored or not.

drop-ins: This contains a list of the unit's drop-in files. Each unit information set contains *name*, which specifies the unit's drop-in files, and *content*, which is plain text representing the unit's drop-in file.

The following is a sample unit configuration in the cloud-config file:

```
#cloud-config
  units:
    - name: etcd2.service
      command: start
    - name: fleet.service
      command: start
    - name: docker-tcp.socket
      command: start
      enable: true
      content: |
        [Unit]
        Description=Docker Socket for the API

        [Socket]
        ListenStream=2375
        Service=docker.service
        BindIPv6Only=both

        [Install]
        WantedBy=sockets.target
```

- `ssh_authorized_keys`: This parameter specifies the public SSH keys that will be authorized for the core user.

- `hostname`: This specifies the hostname of the member.

- `users`: This specifies the list of users to be created or updated on the member. Each user information contains name, password, homedir, shell, and so on.

- `write_files`: This specifies the list of files that are to be created on the member. Each file information contains path, permission, owner, content, and so on.

- `manage_etc_hosts`: This specifies the content of the `/etc/hosts` file for local name resolution. Currently, only localhost is supported.

The config.rb configuration file

This file contains information to configure the CoreOS cluster. This file provides the configuration value for the parameters used by `Vagrantfile`. `Vagrantfile` accesses the configuration by including the `config.rb` file. The following are the parameters:

- `$num_instances`: This parameter specifies the number of nodes in the cluster

- `$shared_folders`: This parameter specifies the list of shared folder paths on the host machine along with the respective path on the member

- `$forwarded_ports`: This specifies the port forwarding from the member to the host machine

- `$vm_gui`: This flag specifies if GUI is to be set up for the member

- `$vm_memory`: This parameter specifies the memory for the member in MBs

- `$vm_cpus`: This specifies the number of CPUs to be allocated for the member

- `$instance_name_prefix`: This parameter specifies the prefix to be used for the member name

- `$update_channel`: This parameter specifies the update channel (alpha, beta, and so on) for CoreOS

The following is a sample `config.rb` file:

```
$num_instances=1
$new_discovery_url="https://discovery.etcd.io/new?size=#{$num_
instances}"

# To automatically replace the discovery token on 'vagrant up',
uncomment
# the lines below:
#
#if File.exists?('user-data') && ARGV[0].eql?('up')
```

```
#   require 'open-uri'
#   require 'yaml'
#
#   token = open($new_discovery_url).read
#
#   data = YAML.load(IO.readlines('user-data')[1..-1].join)
#   if data['coreos'].key? 'etcd'
#     data['coreos']['etcd']['discovery'] = token
#   end
#   if data['coreos'].key? 'etcd2'
#     data['coreos']['etcd2']['discovery'] = token
#   end
#
#   # Fix for YAML.load() converting reboot-strategy from 'off' to
      false`
#   if data['coreos']['update'].key? 'reboot-strategy'
#      if data['coreos']['update']['reboot-strategy'] == false
#           data['coreos']['update']['reboot-strategy'] = 'off'
#       end
#   end
#
#   yaml = YAML.dump(data)
#   File.open('user-data', 'w') { |file| file.write("#cloud-
      config\n\n#{yaml}") }
#end

$instance_name_prefix="coreOS-learn"
$image_version = "current"
$update_channel='alpha'
$vm_gui = false
$vm_memory = 1024
$vm_cpus = 1
$shared_folders = {}
$forwarded_ports = {}
```

Starting a CoreOS VM using Vagrant

Once the config.rb and user-config files are updated with the actual
configuration parameter, execute the command vagrant up in the directory where
configuration files are present to start the CoreOS VM image. Once the vagrant up
command is successfully executed, the CoreOS in the VM environment is ready:

```
vagrant up

Bringing machine 'core-01' up with 'virtualbox' provider...

==> core-01: Checking if box 'coreos-alpha' is up to date...

==> core-01: Clearing any previously set forwarded ports...

==> core-01: Clearing any previously set network interfaces...
```

```
==> core-01: Preparing network interfaces based on configuration...
    core-01: Adapter 1: nat
    core-01: Adapter 2: hostonly
==> core-01: Forwarding ports...
    core-01: 22 => 2222 (adapter 1)
==> core-01: Running 'pre-boot' VM customizations...
==> core-01: Booting VM...
==> core-01: Waiting for machine to boot. This may take a few minutes...
    core-01: SSH address: 127.0.0.1:2222
    core-01: SSH username: core
    core-01: SSH auth method: private key
    core-01: Warning: Connection timeout. Retrying...
==> core-01: Machine booted and ready!
==> core-01: Setting hostname...
==> core-01: Configuring and enabling network interfaces...
==> core-01: Machine already provisioned. Run `vagrant provision` or
             use the `--provision`
==> core-01: flag to force provisioning. Provisioners marked to run
             always will still run.


vagrant status
Current machine states:


core-01                      running (virtualbox)
```

The VM is running. To stop this VM, you can run `vagrant halt` to shut it down forcefully, or you can run `vagrant suspend` to simply suspend the virtual machine. In either case, to restart it again, simply run `vagrant up`.

Setting up CoreOS on VMware vSphere

VMware vSphere is a server virtualization platform that uses VMware's ESX/ESXi hypervisor. VMware VSphere provides complete platform, toolsets and virtualization infrastructure to provide and manage virtual machines in bare metal. VMware vSphere consists of VMware vCenter Server and VMware vSphere Client. VMware vCenter Server manages the virtual as well as the physical resources. VMware vSphere Client provides a GUI to install and manage virtual machines in bare metal.

Installing VMware vSphere Client

Download the latest version of VMware vSphere Client installation as per the host operating system and architecture from `http://vsphereclient.vmware.com/vsphereclient/1/9/9/3/0/7/2/VMware-viclient-all-5.5.0-1993072.exe`. After the download is complete, start the installation. During installation, continue with the default options.

Once the installation is complete, open the VMware vSphere Client application. This opens a new GUI. In the **IP address** / **Name** field, enter the IP address/hostname to directly manage a single host. Enter the IP address/hostname of vCenter Server to manage multiple hosts. In the **User name** and **Password** field, enter the username and password.

Download the latest version of the CoreOS image from `http://stable.release.core-os.net/amd64-usr/current/coreos_production_vmware_ova.ova`. Once the download is complete, the next step is to create the VM image using the downloaded `ova` file. The steps to create the VM image are as follows:

1. Open the VMware vSphere Client application.

2. Enter IP address, username and password as mentioned earlier.

3. Click on the **File** menu.

4. Click on **Deploy OVF Template**.

5. This opens a new Wizard. Specify the location of the `ova` file that was downloaded earlier. Click on **Next.**

6. Specify the name of the VM and inventory location in the **Name and Location** tab.

7. Specify the host/server where this VM is to be deployed in the **Host/Cluster** tab.

8. Specify the location where the VM image should be stored in the **Storage** tab.

9. Specify the disk format in the **Disk Format** tab.

10. Click on **Next**. It takes a while to deploy the VM image.

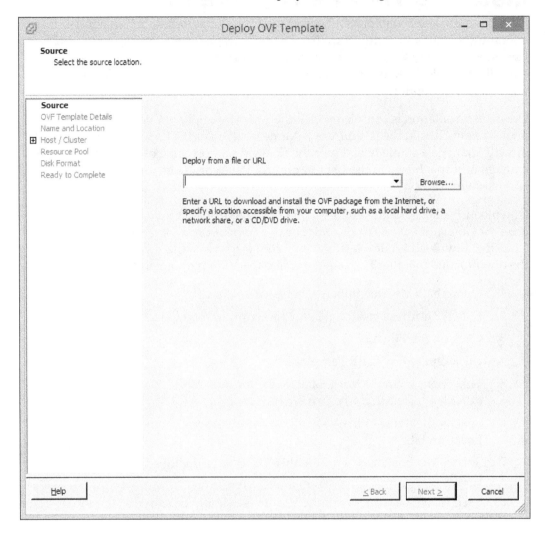

Once the VM image is deployed in the VMware server, we need to start the CoreOS VM with the appropriate cloud-config file having required configuration property. The cloud-config file in VMware vSphere should be specified by attaching a config-drive which is an iso file with filesystem labeled config-2 by attaching CD-ROMs or new drives. The following are the commands to create the iso file in a Linux-based operating system:

1. Create a folder, say /tmp/new-drive/openstack/latest, as follows:

```
mkdir -p /tmp/new-drive/openstack/latest
```

2. Copy the `user_data` file, which is the `cloud-config` file, into the folder:

   `cp user_data /tmp/new-drive/openstack/latest/user_data`

3. Create the `iso` file using the command `mkisofs` as follows:

   `mkisofs -R -V config-2 -o configdrive.iso /tmp/new-drive`

Once the `config-drive` file is created, perform the following steps to attach the `config` file to the VM:

1. Transfer the `iso` image to the machine wherein the VMware vSphere Client program is running.

2. Open VMware vSphere Client.

3. Click on the CoreOS VM and go to the **Summary** tab of the VM as shown in the following screenshot:

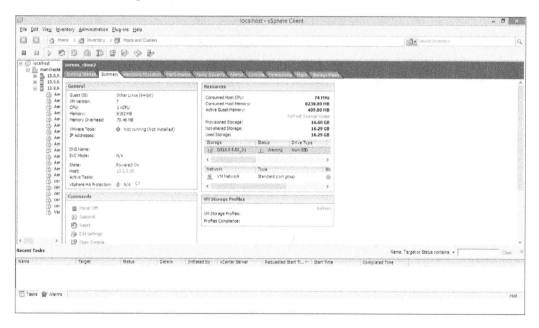

4. Right-click over the **Datastore** section and click on **Browse Datastore**. This will open a new window called **Datastore Browser**.

5. Select the folder named `iso`.

6. Click on the **Upload file to Datastore** icon.

7. Select the `iso` file in the local machine and upload the `iso` file to the **Datastore**.

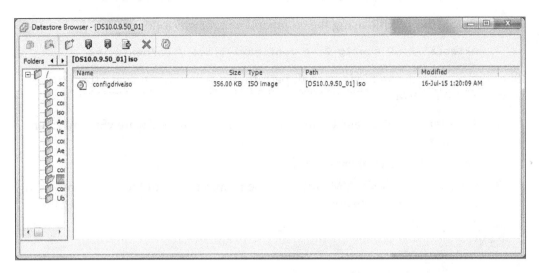

The next step is to attach the `iso` file as a `cloud-config` file for the VM. Perform the following steps:

1. Go to **CoreOS VM** and right-click.

2. Click on **Properties**.

3. Select **CD/DVD drive 1**.

4. On the right-hand side, select **Device Status** as **Connected** as well as **Connect at power on**.

5. Click on **Datastore ISO File** and select the uploaded `iso` file from the data store.

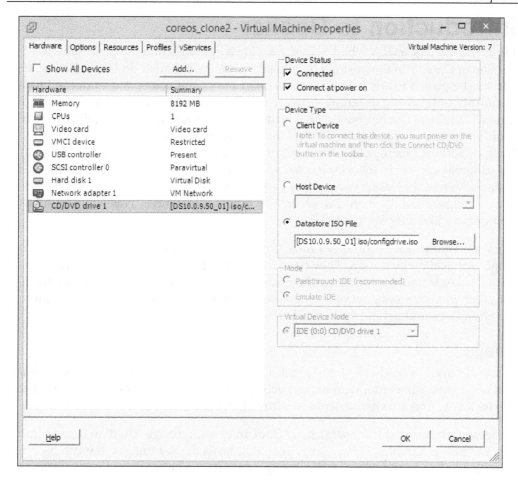

Once the `iso` file is uploaded and attached to the VM, start the VM. The CoreOS VM the VMware environment is ready.

Introduction to Docker

Linux Containers, as described before, provide a lightweight or stripped-down version of OS within the host OS. Applications can be installed on Linux Containers and can be ported to any host OS supporting Linux Containers. A user doesn't have to care about releasing different software for different target machines. Multiple Linux Containers can be created on a host OS, thus providing the capability to run multiple instances of software on the same machine independent of each other. Imagine software using a large number of ports and a tedious configuration file. In a traditional approach, the user has to carefully create the configuration file for each instance so that they don't conflict with another instance. In Linux Containers, the same configuration file would work on all Container instances. This helps with faster deployment and simpler operation.

Docker containers are primarily Linux Containers that are capable of running a single application by design. They have the capability to run on any machine with Docker installed. Docker can be installed over a variety of machines running different operating systems such as Linux or Mac and thus making the application portable. Let's understand some Docker concepts.

Image

Docker image is a read-only template. Usually, images contain an OS snapshot, but Docker images can contain anything, such as a database and OS or application. They are read only and are shared across multiple Docker containers.

Images can be created from scratch, or from an existing image listed on docker hub. **Docker hub** is a public `Docker Registry` that hosts docker images that can be downloaded and used. We can also set up a private docker registry.

Images have a unique ID and a unique human-readable name and tag pair. Images can be called, for example, `ubuntu:latest`, `ubuntu:precise`, `django:1.6`, `django:1.7`, and so on.

Docker uses **Union File System** to combine layers of images to form a single Docker image. Union File System allows files and directories in different filesystems to be overlaid over a single filesystem. A docker image starts with the base image, usually a standard OS image over which other layers of images are appended. Each layer provides additional functionalities over the previous layers. Upon image changes, only impact layers need to be provided instead of the complete image.

Container

Containers are created from the Docker Image. Container holds everything required for an application to run, such as user files, metadata, user applications, and so on. To expose the service provided by the containers, Docker allows exposing specific ports of a container.

Volumes

As described before, Docker images are layers of read-only Union filesystems. When we start a container, additionally a read-write layer is created over the top of the read-only layer as there may be a requirement to modify a file (for instance). When some modification is made, data is present in both the read-write and read-only layers. This is required so that the image used in the container remains unchanged. The scope of this read-write layer is only until the container exists. Once the container is deleted, the read-write layer is destroyed and the read-only (unchanged) image is available for reuse. **Volumes** provide a mechanism to manage data within and across containers. They also provide a mechanism to share data from the host machine to the container, thus enabling data to be outside the container. Data can be directly shared from the host folder or from another container. It's recommended to create a data-only container and share data from that container.

Links

Docker containers can connect to each other using the network port mappings created while containers are created. This brings some element of hardcoding as the ports are preconfigured. Container links can also be used by linking the source container to the recipient container using container names. Docker exposes connectivity information for the source container to the recipient container through environment variables and by modifying the /etc/hosts file. The environment variables are prefixed with the link name and follow naming convention to help the recipient identify the interface details (such as protocol used, IP address, port, and so on). The /etc/hosts file is updated with the source container IP address and the hostname as the container name.

Installing Docker

Docker can also be installed on a variety of platforms, virtual machines and cloud providers. Docker contains two components:

- Docker Client: The user invokes Docker Client to start, stop, and manage the Docker container.
- Docker Daemon: Docker Client interfaces with Docker Daemon to actually start, stop, and manage the Docker container. Docker Daemon can only run on Linux machines. So if Docker is installed on Windows or Mac, Docker Daemon runs inside Linux Virtual Machine (for instance, in VirtualBox).

There are two ways to create a Docker image:

- Using Docker File and the Docker build command
- Using the pre-built docker images from dockerhub

Creating a sample Docker image using Docker File

In this section, we will learn how to create Docker containers through Docker File. Docker File has obvious benefits. Docker File helps automate the build process, it can be version controlled for the project, and inline comments serve as help for beginners and many others.

The following is the simple Docker File that creates a docker image using the CentOS base image:

```
$cat Dockerfile
FROM centos
CMD ["uname", "-a"]


$ docker build -t docker_uname .
Sending build context to Docker daemon 2.048 kB
Step 0 : FROM centos
 ---> 7322fbe74aa5
Step 1 : CMD uname -a
 ---> Using cache
 ---> 36d993cf27b9
Successfully built 36d993cf27b9
```

Docker File

Docker File contains the instructions used by Docker to build the images. The Docker File takes the following format:

```
# Comment
INSTRUCTION arguments
```

The instructions are run in order. The lines beginning with # are treated as comments and are not executed. Environment variables can also be used as variables in instruction arguments. Some of the important instructions are:

- FROM: This sets the base image for the Docker image. This is the first instruction. Arguments can be in any one of the following format:

  FROM <image>

  FROM <image>:<tag>

  FROM <image>@<digest>

  If tag or digest is not provided, the latest image is selected.

- RUN: This instruction specifies the commands to be executed for building the container. Typical usages of RUN instructions are updating the base image with OS patches, installing specific packages, updating system configuration, and so on. Each command runs in a separate layer on top of the current image and committed. The committed image is then used for the next step. Arguments can be in any one of the following format:

  RUN <command>

  In this form, command is executed within shell /bin/sh -c. Shell /bin/sh -c is the default ENTRYPOINT for docker:

  RUN ["executable", "param1", "param2"]

  In this form, command is executed directly without invoking a shell.

- ENTRYPOINT: This specifies the executable and its corresponding parameters when docker is started. Any parameters that are passed during the starting of docker are appended to ENTRYPOINT and executed.

  Arguments can be in any one of the following formats:

  - ENTRYPOINT ["executable", "param1", "param2"]: In this format, command is executed directly without invoking a shell.

  - ENTRYPOINT <command> <paramters>: In this format, command is executed within shell /bin/sh -c.

- CMD: This specifies the defaults (that is, executable, shell, and command-line parameters) for the containers to be executed when docker is started. This is different from RUN as RUN instructions are only executed during building an image.

  Arguments can be in any one of the following format:

  - CMD ["executable","param1","param2"]: This format is used when ENTRYPOINT is not provided. Command is executed here without a shell.

  - CMD ["param1","param2"]: This format is used when ENTRYPOINT is provided with a default command. The parameters provided here are appended to ENTRYPOINT and executed.

  - CMD command param1 param2 (shell form): In this format, command is executed within shell /bin/sh -c.

  Only one CMD instruction is executed. If multiple CMD instructions are provided, the last instruction is used.

- EXPOSE: This specifies the list of listening ports on which Docker is listening. The format of this field is: EXPOSE <port> [<port>...]

- VOLUME: This specifies the mount path in the container and the external directories from the host machine or volumes from another container. The format of this field is: VOLUME <directory> [<directory>...]

Pulling the Docker image from Docker Hub

Docker Hub is a community-driven docker image hosting service provided by Docker that has capabilities for public and private content. Already there are more than 100,000 images available in the Docker Hub registry. Instead of building docker images using Docker File, docker images can be directly downloaded from Docker Hub. The docker pull command is used to pull the images directly from Docker Hub and the format is as follows:

```
docker pull centos
```

Running Docker Image

Let's start by running an already existing system command from the Docker container. The Docker container in this example prints the system information and exits:

```
$ docker run centos uname -a
Linux 3c954433a1e2 4.0.9-boot2docker #1 SMP Thu Aug 13 03:05:44 UTC
2015 x86_64 x86_64 x86_64 GNU/Linux
```

The run parameter runs Docker containers. The image name is provided as centos. During the first run, if the image is not available in the local machine, the latest-version centos image is downloaded from the public image registry Docker Hub. Since no version of the image was specified, the latest version was chosen. If a specific version is required to be installed, it can also be provided, for example, centos:6.6. The uname -a command is then executed inside the container using the default ENTRYPOINT /bin/sh -c. After the command execution is completed, the container exits.

We will create a more sophisticated Docker File container that executes the RUN instruction to install a package over the base image and listens for a TCP connection:

```
$cat Dockerfile
FROM centos


# install ncat commad to be used for this demo during build. Ncat
# is not part of standard package.
RUN ["yum", "-y", "install", "nc"]


# print machine ips
RUN ["cat", "/etc/hosts"]


# run the command ncat to listen on all IP address on port 12345
CMD ["ncat", "-vv", "-l", "0.0.0.0", "12345"]


$ docker build -t dock_ncat .
Sending build context to Docker daemon 3.072 kB
Step 0 : FROM centos
 ---> 7322fbe74aa5
Step 1 : RUN yum -y install nc
 ---> Using cache
 ---> 886063e43760
Step 2 : RUN cat /etc/hosts
 ---> Using cache
 ---> df623793d532
Step 3 : CMD ncat -vv -l 0.0.0.0 12345
 ---> Running in a0a5daa581b4
 ---> f8ad341c047e
```

```
Removing intermediate container a0a5daa581b4

Successfully built f8ad341c047e Removing intermediate container
6f8284dad1f8

Successfully built 3c60a690a2d7



$ docker run -p :12344:12345 dock_ncat

Ncat: Version 6.40 ( http://nmap.org/ncat )

Ncat: Listening on 0.0.0.0:12345

Ncat: Connection from 172.18.42.1.

Ncat: Connection from 172.18.42.1:58939.
```

Port `12345` from the container is mapped to port `12344` on the host. If the host tries
to connect on `12344`, a connection gets established on the container.

Summary

In this chapter, we were able to set up and run CoreOS with a single machine
using Vagrant and VirtualBox. We were also able to create and run Docker images.
In due process, we familiarized ourselves with the important configuration files
and their contents.

In the next chapter, we will learn how to set up a CoreOS cluster with multiple
machines. We will also learn how machines are discovered and services are
scheduled on those machines.

3
Creating Your CoreOS Cluster and Managing the Cluster

This chapter covers CoreOS clustering, providing information on the concepts and benefits of clustering. We will also learn how to set up clusters and get familiar with all the services involved in clustering with greater detail.

This chapter covers the following topics:

- Introduction to clustering
- The why and the benefits of clustering
- CoreOS clustering
- Creating a CoreOS cluster
- Discovery using etcd
- Systemd
- Service deployment and High Availability (HA) using fleet

Introduction to clustering

There are two ways to scale a system. One is to scale vertically, that is, by adding more hardware resources to a machine. If the memory requirement of the system increases, add more memory; if more processing is required, upgrade the machine to one using higher-end processors or providing a higher number of cores. Horizontal scaling is another way to scale a system to higher capacity. This means adding more machines when required to form a cluster of nodes. This cluster of nodes work in tandem to provide service. The nodes in the cluster may have applications performing the same role like a pool or they may perform a different role.

The why and the benefits of clustering

Horizontal scalability of a system is limited by hardware resources available in the market. For instance, scaling up RAM from 8 GB to 32 or 64 GB may be cost effective, as many products may be commonly available, but increasing it further may be cost inhibitive. Similarly, scaling up CPU is also limited by system configuration available in the market. Further doubling the hardware capability doesn't result in equal performance improvements. It's typically less.

With virtualization and cloud services, the cost of buying and maintaining hardware is coming down, making vertical scaling or clustering or scaling out more is lucrative. The increased performance of communication networks has considerably reduced the latency in the communication of nodes in the cluster. Clustering has various advantages, such as:

- **On-demand scaling**: The nodes in the cluster can be added as and when required. We can start with a dimensioned system and keep on adding nodes as capacity increases.

- **Dynamic scaling**: Most of the clustering solutions provide a mechanism to add/remove nodes at runtime. Hence, the system as a whole will be up and running for providing service while cluster modifications are being performed.

- **Redundancy**: A cluster can be configured with few spare nodes. Upon failure of any nodes or during planned or unplanned maintenance of nodes, these spare nodes can be assigned to the role of the failed node or nodes under maintenance without impacting service capacity.

It's also important to know about the shortcomings of clusters to make an informed decision while architecting a system. As the number of nodes increase, the complexity in the management of those nodes also increases. All the nodes need to be monitored and maintained. The software also has to be designed to be able to run on multiple nodes. There comes a requirement for an orchestration mechanism to orchestrate the applications across different instances in the cluster. For instance, load balancers to distribute load across worker nodes, or job serializers to synchronize and serialize a job across nodes.

CoreOS clustering

Chapter 1, CoreOS, Yet Another Linux Distro covers CoreOS cluster architecture. We will summarize it here again. A CoreOS member or node can contain multiple Docker containers. There can be multiple CoreOS members forming a CoreOS cluster.

CoreOS uses fleet to schedule and manage the services using `systemd` onto the CoreOS members during initialization. This is similar to the `systemd` starting and managing service on Linux machines. The scope of the Linux `systemd` process is limited to a host node, whereas CoreOS `fleetd` is the init system for a complete CoreOS cluster.

CoreOS uses etcd for node discovery and storing key-value pairs of configuration items accessible across a cluster member.

It's possible to set up a cluster in two ways:

- **etcd running on all members**: When the number of members of the cluster is few, then etcd can be run on all the members running the services, also called workers. This configuration is simpler as the same `cloud-config` can be used to start all the members of the cluster.

- **etcd running on few members**: When the number of members in the cluster is large, typically greater than ten, it is advisable to run `etcd` and other CoreOS cluster services exclusively on some of the machines. This becomes easier to dimension the platform configuration of the worker members as they are exclusively used for providing services. In this, two `cloud-config` files are required: one for CoreOS cluster services including etcd, and the other for workers or proxies.

The setting of CoreOS clusters is fairly simple. Prepare the `cloud-config` file and start booting members using the file. Small scripting knowledge is required to regenerate the configuration files per member. The discovery service and etcd use the discovery token or static token provided to form a cluster as the members are started.

Cluster discovery

This section describes the various discovery mechanisms used by CoreOS to form a cluster. For the examples in this chapter, the following is the system configuration:

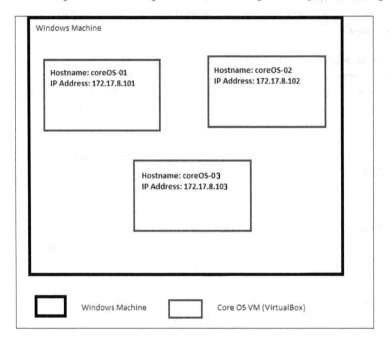

Static discovery

The **static discovery** mechanism is used when the IP addresses of the members are known beforehand. IPs are preconfigured in the cloud-config file. They are useful in scenarios where the cluster size is small and can be generally used for test setups. Configuring large numbers of hardcoded IPs will be error prone and a maintenance nightmare.

The following is the cloud-config file that is used to create a cluster using static discovery:

```
#cloud-config

---
coreos:
  etcd2:
```

```
name: core-01
advertise-client-urls: http://$public_ipv4:2379
initial-advertise-peer-urls: http://$private_ipv4:2380
listen-client-urls: http://0.0.0.0:2379,http://0.0.0.0:4001
listen-peer-urls:
http://$private_ipv4:2380,http://$private_ipv4:7001
initial-cluster-token: coreOS-static
initial-cluster: core-01=http://172.17.8.101:2380,core-
02=http://172.17.8.102:2380,core-03=http://172.17.8.103:2380
units:
- name: etcd2.service
command: start
enable: true
```

There are two new fields that were not discussed before. The name field provides the name of the member. This is also used to correlate the member to the URL in initial-cluster. The initial-cluster field provides the member name and URL of all the members of the cluster.

The IP addresses provided in the initial-cluster field should contain the static IP address.

In order to create the previously mentioned cloud-config file, for all the nodes that want to be part of the cluster, the following steps need to be performed.

Vagrantfile should contain static IP addresses allocated to each member. As shown in the following sample, IP 172.17.8.101 is assigned to the first member, IP 172.17.8.102 is assigned to the second member, and so on:

```
...
    ip = "172.17.8.#{i+100}"
    config.vm.network :private_network, ip: ip
...
```

You might have noticed the cloud-config file contains the name of only one member, but the systemd unit file for the etcd service in each CoreOS VM should contain its own member name. This requires the following instrumentation in Vagrantfile to generate the cloud-config file specific to each member. Without going into the specifics of ruby, the following code modifies the name parameter for each member and stores in a separate file.

The generated file is `user-data-1` for the first member, `user-data-2` for the second member, and so on. Except for the `name` field, all other parameters are used from the `cloud-config` file provided. The generated files are used during boot-up of Virtual Machines:

```
    . . .
        if $share_home
          config.vm.synced_folder ENV['HOME'], ENV['HOME'], id: "home",
  :nfs => true, :mount_options => ['nolock,vers=3,udp']
        end

        if File.exist?(CLOUD_CONFIG_PATH)
          user_data_specific = "#{CLOUD_CONFIG_PATH}-#{i}"
          require 'yaml'
          data = YAML.load(IO.readlines(CLOUD_CONFIG_PATH)[1..-
  1].join)
          if data['coreos'].key? 'etcd2'
            data['coreos']['etcd2']['name'] = vm_name
          end
          yaml = YAML.dump(data)
          File.open(user_data_specific, 'w') { |file|
          file.write("#cloud-config\n\n#{yaml}") }
          config.vm.provision :file, :source => user_data_specific,
          :destination => "/tmp/vagrantfile-user-data"
          config.vm.provision :shell, :inline => "mv
          /tmp/vagrantfile-user-data /var/lib/coreos-vagrant/",
          :privileged => true
        end
    . . .
```

Set `$num_instances` to `3` in the `config.rb` file and setup is complete for a three-member cluster:

Boot the cluster using `Vagrant up`. Upon successful boot-up, we can see the members of the cluster.

```
vagrant ssh core-01
```

```
etcdctl member list
7cc8bd52fa88d49: name=core-02 peerURLs=http://172.17.8.102:2380 clientURL
s=http://172.17.8.102:2379

533d38560a602262: name=core-01 peerURLs=http://172.17.8.101:2380 clientUR
Ls=http://172.17.8.101:2379
```

```
b8d2db3a5bf3d17d: name=core-03 peerURLs=http://172.17.8.103:2380 clientUR
Ls=http://172.17.8.103:2379


etcdctl cluster-health
cluster is healthy
member 533d38560a602262 is healthy
member 7cc8bd52fa88d49 is healthy
member b8d2db3a5bf3d17d is healthy
```

etcd discovery

The etcd discovery mechanism is used when the IP addresses of the members are not known in advance or DHCP is used to assign IP addresses. There can be two modes of discovery: public and custom.

If the cluster has access to the public IP, the public discovery service discovery. etcd.io can be used to generate a token and manage cluster membership. Access the website https://discovery.etcd.io/new?size=<clustersize> and generate a token. Note that cluster size is required to be provided while generating a token.

Generation of a token can be automated in the config.rb file by uncommenting the following lines:

```
. . .
# To automatically replace the discovery token on 'vagrant up',
uncomment
# the lines below:
#
```

```
if File.exists?('user-data') && ARGV[0].eql?('up')
  require 'open-uri'
  require 'yaml'

  token = open($new_discovery_url).read

  data = YAML.load(IO.readlines('user-data')[1..-1].join)

  if data['coreos'].key? 'etcd2'
    data['coreos']['etcd2']['discovery'] = token
  end

  yaml = YAML.dump(data)
  File.open('user-data', 'w') { |file| file.write("#cloud-
  config\n\n#{yaml}") }
end
...
```

The following is the cloud-config file that is used to create a cluster using public etcd discovery:

```
#cloud-config

coreos:
  etcd2:
    discovery: https://discovery.etcd.io/<token>
    advertise-client-urls: http://$public_ipv4:2379
    initial-advertise-peer-urls: http://$private_ipv4:2380
    listen-client-urls: http://0.0.0.0:2379,http://0.0.0.0:4001
    listen-peer-urls:
    http://$private_ipv4:2380,http://$private_ipv4:7001
  units:
    - name: etcd2.service
      command: start
      enable: true
```

Set $num_instances to 3 in the config.rb file and setup is complete for a three-member cluster. Compared to static discovery, this is a simpler process and no instrumentation is required in Vagrantfile.

Boot the cluster using `Vagrant up`. Upon successful boot-up, we can see the members of the cluster:

```
vagrant ssh core-01

etcdctl member list
466abd73fa498e31: name=5fd5fe90fef243a090cb2ee4cfac4d53 peerURLs=ht
tp://172.17.8.103:2380 clientURLs=http://172.17.8.103:2379
940245793b93afb3: name=43e78c85f5bb439f84badd8a5cb9f12b peerURLs=ht
tp://172.17.8.101:2380 clientURLs=http://172.17.8.101:2379
ea07891f96c6abfe: name=93c559a5c40d47c7917607a15d676b6d peerURLs=ht
tp://172.17.8.102:2380 clientURLs=http://172.17.8.102:2379


etcdctl cluster-health
cluster is healthy
member 466abd73fa498e31 is healthy
member 940245793b93afb3 is healthy
member ea07891f96c6abfe is healthy
```

Instead of using a public discovery, an `etcd` instance can be used as the discovery service to manage cluster membership. One of the `etcd` instances is configured with the token and number of cluster instances and other `etcd` instances use it to join to the cluster.

The following is the `cloud-config` file that is used to create a cluster using public `etcd` discovery:

```
#cloud-config

coreos:
  etcd2:
    discovery:
    http://172.17.8.101:4001/v2/keys/discovery/40134540-b53c-46b3-
    b34f-33b4f0ae3a9c
    advertise-client-urls: http://$public_ipv4:2379
    initial-advertise-peer-urls: http://$private_ipv4:2380
    listen-client-urls:
    http://$public_ipv4:2379,http://$public_ipv4:4001
    listen-peer-urls:
    http://$private_ipv4:2380,http://$private_ipv4:7001
  units:
    - name: etcd2.service
      command: start
      enable: true
```

The token can be generated using the `uuidgen` Linux command. The path `v2/keys/discovery` is where cluster information is stored. Any path can be provided. Machine one is used as the custom discovery node.

The `etcd` service running on machine one doesn't need a discovery token since it is not going to be part of the cluster. This requires the following instrumentation in `Vagrantfile` to generate the `cloud-config` file separately for machine one and other machines. The following code modifies the name parameter for each member, removes unwanted parameters for machine one, and stores in a separate file for each member. In the following sample, the parameters that are not required are set to empty; they can be deleted:

```
    . . .
        if $share_home
            config.vm.synced_folder ENV['HOME'], ENV['HOME'], id: "home",
    :nfs => true,  :mount_options => ['nolock,vers=3,udp']
        end

        if File.exist?(CLOUD_CONFIG_PATH)
          user_data_specific = "#{CLOUD_CONFIG_PATH}-#{i}"
          require 'yaml'
          data = YAML.load(IO.readlines(CLOUD_CONFIG_PATH)[1..-
          1].join)
          if data['coreos'].key? 'etcd2'
            data['coreos']['etcd2']['name'] = vm_name
          end
          if i.equal? 1
            data['coreos']['etcd2']['discovery'] = nil
            data['coreos']['etcd2']['initial-advertise-peer-urls']
            = nil
            data['coreos']['etcd2']['listen-peer-urls'] = nil
          end
          yaml = YAML.dump(data)
          File.open(user_data_specific, 'w') { |file|
          file.write("#cloud-config\n\n#{yaml}") }
          config.vm.provision :file, :source => user_data_specific,
          :destination => "/tmp/vagrantfile-user-data"
          config.vm.provision :shell, :inline => "mv
          /tmp/vagrantfile-user-data /var/lib/coreos-vagrant/",
          :privileged => true
        end
    . . .
```

Set $num_instances to 3 in the config.rb file and boot the cluster using Vagrant up. Initially, the cluster formation will fail as the number of nodes corresponding to the discovery token is not set. Set the number of nodes as 2 in the cluster. The path provided in the discovery token URL should match the path provided in the URL.

```
vagrant ssh core-01

curl -X PUT http://172.17.8.101:4001/v2/keys/discovery/40134540-b53c-
46b3-b34f-33b4f0ae3a9c/_config/size -d value=2
```

```
{"action":"set","node":{"key":"/discovery/40134540-b53c-46b3-b34f-
33b4f0ae3a9c/_config/size","value":"2","modifiedIndex":3,"createdInd
ex":3}}
```

Upon setting the node size, we can see the members in the cluster. This time, we additionally need to provide the endpoint information on which etcd is listening as the cloud-config file contains a specific IP address instead of wildcard IPs in the previous examples:

```
etcdctl --peers=http://172.17.8.102:4001 member list
36b2390cc35b7932: name=core-03 peerURLs=http://172.17.8.103:2380 clien
tURLs=http://172.17.8.103:2379
654398796d95b9a6: name=core-02 peerURLs=http://172.17.8.102:2380 clien
tURLs=http://172.17.8.102:2379

etcdctl --peers=http://172.17.8.102:4001 cluster-health
cluster is healthy
member 36b2390cc35b7932 is healthy
member 654398796d95b9a6 is healthy
```

DNS discovery

Cluster discovery can also be performed using DNS SRV records. Contact your system administrator to create DNS SRV records to map the hostname to the service. DNS A records should also be created to map the hostname to the IP address of the members.

The DNS domain name containing the discovery SRV records is required to be provided using the discovery-srv parameter. The following DNS SRV records are looked up in the listed order:

- _etcd-server-ssl._tcp.<domain name>
- _etcd-server._tcp.<domain name>

If _etcd-server-ssl._tcp.<domain name> is found then etcd will attempt the bootstrapping process over SSL.

The following SRV and DNS A records are to be created:

```
_etcd-server._tcp.testdomain.com. 300     IN        SRV       0         0
2380      CoreOS-01.testdomain.com.
_etcd-server._tcp.testdomain.com. 300     IN        SRV       0         0
2380      CoreOS-02.testdomain.com.
_etcd-server._tcp.testdomain.com. 300     IN        SRV       0         0
2380      CoreOS-03.testdomain.com.
CoreOS-01.testdomain.com.             300       IN        A         172.17.8.101
CoreOS-02.testdomain.com.             300       IN        A         172.17.8.102
CoreOS-03.testdomain.com.             300       IN        A         172.17.8.103
```

The following is the cloud-config file that is used to create a cluster using public etcd discovery:

```
#cloud-config
coreos:
  etcd2:
    discovery-srv: testdomain.com
    advertise-client-urls: http://$public_ipv4:2379
    initial-advertise-peer-urls: http://$private_ipv4:2380
    listen-client-urls: http://0.0.0.0:2379,http://0.0.0.0:4001
    listen-peer-urls:
    http://$private_ipv4:2380,http://$private_ipv4:7001
    initial-cluster-token: etcd-cluster-1
    initial-cluster-state: new
  units:
  - name: etcd2.service
    command: start
    enable: true
write_files:
  - path: "/etc/resolv.conf"
    permissions: "0644"
    owner: "root"
    content: |
      nameserver 172.17.8.111
```

 The cloud-config file contains additional section write-files to point to the DNS server where SRV and A records are created.

Set $num_instances to 3 in the config.rb file and setup is complete for a three-member cluster. Compared to static discovery, this is a simpler process and no instrumentation is required in Vagrantfile.

Boot the cluster using Vagrant up. Upon successful boot-up, we can see the members of the cluster:

```
vagrant ssh core-01

etcdctl member list
13530017c40ce74f: name=5d0c2805e0944d43b03ef260fea20ae2
peerURLs=http://CoreOS-02.testdomain.com:2380 clientURLs=ht
tp://172.17.8.102:2379
25c0879f38e80fd0: name=26fed2d2c43b4901ad944d9912d071cb
peerURLs=http://CoreOS-01.testdomain.com:2380 clientURLs=ht
tp://172.17.8.101:2379
3551738c55e6c3e4: name=39d95e1e69ae4bea97aed0ba5817241e
peerURLs=http://CoreOS-03.testdomain.com:2380 clientURLs=ht
tp://172.17.8.103:2379

etcdctl cluster-health
member 13530017c40ce74f is healthy: got healthy result from
http://172.17.8.102:2379
member 25c0879f38e80fd0 is healthy: got healthy result from
http://172.17.8.101:2379
member 3551738c55e6c3e4 is healthy: got healthy result from
http://172.17.8.103:2379
cluster is healthy
```

systemd

systemd is an init system that most of the Linux distribution, including CoreOS, has adopted to start other services/daemons during boot-up. systemd is designed to run multiple operations required to start services in parallel, resulting in faster boot-up. systemd manages services, devices, sockets, disk mounts, and so on, called units. systemd performs operations like start, stop, enable, and disable on the units. Each unit has a corresponding configuration file called **unit file** that contains information about actions to be performed for each operation, dependencies on other units, execution pre-conditions and post-conditions, and so on.

In this section, we will understand how to configure a service using unit file and perform basic operations on the services. Let's start by understanding the contents of unit file.

Service unit files

Unit files are embedded in the `cloud-config` file and CoreOS copies the information verbatim to corresponding unit files.

The unit name must be of the form `string.suffix` or `string@instance.suffix`, where:

- `string` must not be an empty string and can only contain alphanumeric characters and any of `':'`, `'_'`, `'.'`, `'@'`, `'-'`.

- `instance` can be empty, and can only contain the same characters as are valid for `string`.

- `suffix` must be one of the following unit types: `service`, `socket`, `device`, `mount`, `automount`, `timer`, `path`. `service` is used for describing service.

Unit files contain information grouped under sections. Each section contains a list of parameters and their values. Each parameter can occur multiple times in a section. Section and parameter names are case sensitive. As we will be dealing mostly with services, we will discuss configuration relevant to it. The following are the important section names used for services:

- `[Unit]` section: This section is not used by `systemd` and contains information for the user about the service. Some of the important parameters of the `Unit` section are:
    - `Description`: This specifies the description of the service such as name, service provided, and so on.
    - `After`: This specifies service names that are supposed to be started before starting this service.
    - `Before`: This specifies service names that are supposed to be started after starting this service.

- `[Service]` Section: This section contains the configuration for managing units. Some of the important parameters of the `Service` section are:
    - `Type`: This specifies the startup type for the service. The type can be one of the following: `simple`, `forking`, `oneshot`, `dbus`, `notify`, or `idle`.

      The type `simple` indicates that the service is started by executing the command configured in `ExecStart`, and proceeds with other unit file processing. This is the default behavior.

The type `fork` indicates that the parent process will fork a child process and exit upon completion of start. Exiting of the main process is the trigger to process with other unit file processing. To allow systemd to take recovery action upon service failure, the `pid` file containing `pid` if the process providing the service can be configured using `PIDFile`.

The type `oneshot` indicates that the service is started by executing the command configured in `ExecStart`, waits for the exit of the command, and then proceeds with other unit file processing. `RemainAfterExit` can be used to indicate that the service is an active event after the main process has exited.

The type `notify` indicates that the service is started by executing the command configured in `ExecStart`, and waits for the notification using `sd_notify` to indicate startup is complete. Upon notification, `systemd` starts executing other units.

The type `dbus` indicates that the service is started by executing the command configured in `ExecStart`, waits for the service to acquire the D-bus name as specified in `BusName` and then proceeds with other unit file processing.

- ° `TimeoutStartSec`: This specifies the `systemd` wait time during starting the service before marking it as failed.

- ° `ExecStartPre`: This can be used to execute commands before starting the service. This parameter can be provided multiple times in the section to execute multiple commands prior to start. The value contains the full path of the command along with arguments to the command. The value can be preceded by - to indicate that the failure of the command will be ignored and next steps will be executed.

- ° `ExecStart`: This specifies the full path and the arguments of the command to be executed to start the service. If the path to the command is preceded by a dash - character, non-zero exit statuses will be accepted without marking the service activation as failed.

- ° `ExecStartPost`: This can be used to execute commands after starting the service. This parameter can be provided multiple times in the section to execute multiple commands after the start. The value contains the full path of the command along with arguments to the command. The value can be preceded by - to indicate that the failure of the command will be ignored and next steps will be executed.

- ◦ ExecStop: This indicates the command needed to stop the service. If this is not given, the process will be killed immediately when the service is stopped.

- ◦ TimeoutStopSec: This specifies the systemd wait time during stopping the service before forcefully killing it.

- PIDFile: This specifies the absolute filename pointing to the PID file of this service. systemd reads the PID of the main process of the daemon after startup of the service. systemd removes the file after the service has shut down if it still exists.

- BusName: This specifies the D-Bus bus name that this service is reachable at. This option is mandatory for services where Type is set to dbus.

- RemainAfterExit: This flag specifies whether the service shall be considered active even when all its processes exited. Defaults to no.

Starting and stopping a service

systemd provides an interface to monitor and manage the service using the systemctl command. To start a service, invoke the start option with the service name. To start the service permanently after reboot, invoke the enable option with the service name..service can be omitted when the service name is provided to the systemctl command:

```
systemctl enable crond
systemctl start crond
```

To stop the service, invoke the stop option with the service name:

```
systemctl stop crond
```

To check the status of the service, invoke the status option with the service name:

```
systemctl status crond
crond.service - Command Scheduler
   Loaded: loaded (/usr/lib/systemd/system/crond.service; enabled)
   Active: active (running) since Tue 2015-09-08 22:51:30 IST; 2s ago
 Main PID: 8225 (crond)
   CGroup: /system.slice/crond.service
           `-8225 /usr/sbin/crond -n

...
```

fleet

CoreOS extends the init system to the cluster using fleet. fleet emulates all the nodes in the CoreOS cluster to be part of a single init system or system service. fleet controls the systemd service at the cluster level, not at the individual node level, which allows fleet to manage services in any of the nodes in the cluster. fleet handles scheduling a unit/service/container to a cluster member, handles units by rescheduling to another member, and provides an interface for monitoring and managing units locally or remotely. You don't have to care about the coupling of a member to the service, as fleet does it for you. The unit is guaranteed to be running on all the clusters meeting the constraint required for running the service. Unit files are not only limited to launch a Docker, even though most of the time unit files are used to start a Docker. Some of the valid unit types are `.socket`, `.mount`, and so on.

Architectural overview

fleet consists of two main components: **fleet agent** and **fleet engine**. Both these components are part of the `fleetd` module and will be running on all the cluster nodes. Both the engine and agent components work with a reconciliation model, wherein both these components take a snapshot of the current state of the cluster and derive the desired state and try to emulate the derived state of the cluster.

fleet uses the D-Bus interface exposed by systemd. D-Bus is the message bus system for IPC provided by the Linux OS, which provides one-to-one messaging methods and the pub/sub type of message communication.

 As fleet is written in Go language, fleet uses `godbus`, which is the native GO binding for D-Bus.

fleet uses `godbus` to communicate with `systemd` for sending the commands to start/stop units in a particular node. It also uses `godbus` to get the current state of the units periodically.

Engine

The fleetd engine is responsible for making the scheduling decision of the units among the cluster of nodes based on the constraint, if any. The engine talks to etcd for getting the current state of units and nodes in the cluster. All the units, state of the units, and the nodes in the cluster are stored in the etcd data store.

The scheduling decision happens in a timely fashion or is triggered by etcd events. The reconciliation process is triggered by etcd events or time period, wherein the engine takes a snapshot of the current state and the desired state of the cluster, which includes the state of all the units running on the cluster along with the state of all the nodes/agents in the cluster. Based on the current state and desired state of the cluster, it takes necessary action to move from the current state to the desired state and save the desired state as the current state. By default, the engine uses the least-loaded scheduling algorithm, wherein it chooses the node that is loaded less for running a new unit.

Agent

Agent is responsible for starting the units in the node. Once the engines choose the appropriate node for running the units, it is the responsibility of the agent in that node to start the unit. To start the unit, the agent sends start or stop unit commands to the local systemd process using the D-Bus. The agent is also responsible for sending the state of the units to the etcd, which will be later communicated to the engine. Similar to the engine, the agent also runs a periodic reconciler process to compute the current state and desired state of unit files and takes the necessary action to move to the desired state.

The following diagram represents how the job/unit is scheduled by the fleet engine to one of the nodes in the cluster. When the user wants to start a unit using the fleetctl start command, the engine picks this job and adds it to the job offer. The qualified agent running on the node bids for the job on behalf of the node. Once the qualified agent is selected by the engine, it sends the unit to the agent for deployment.

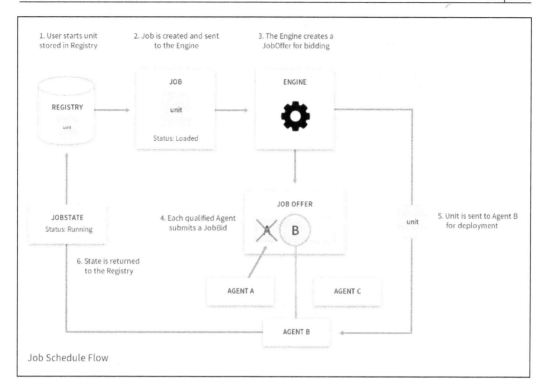

1. User starts unit stored in Registry
2. Job is created and sent to the Engine
3. The Engine creates a JobOffer for bidding

REGISTRY
unit

JOB
unit
Status: Loaded

ENGINE

JOB OFFER

JOBSTATE
Status: Running

4. Each qualified Agent submits a JobBid

5. Unit is sent to Agent B for deployment

unit

6. State is returned to the Registry

AGENT A

AGENT C

AGENT B

Job Schedule Flow

fleetctl

fleetctl is the utility provided by the CoreOS distribution to interface and manage the fleetd module. This is similar to systemctl for systemd to fleet. fleetctl can either be executed on one of the nodes inside the CoreOS cluster or it can be executed on a machine that is not part of the CoreOS cluster. There are different mechanisms to run fleetctl to manage the fleet service.

By default, fleetctl communicates directly with unix:///var/run/fleet.sock, which is a Unix domain socket of the local host machine. To override and to contact a particular node's HTTP API, the --endpoint option should be used, as follows. The --endpoint option can also be provided using FLEETCTL_ENDPOINT environmental options:

```
fleetctl --endpoint http://<IP:PORT> list-units
```

When the user want to execute the fleetctl command from an external machine, the --tunnel option is used, which provides a way to tunnel fleetctl commands to one of the nodes in the cluster using SSH:

```
fleetctl --tunnel 10.0.0.1 list-machines
```

`fleetctl` contains the command to start, stop, and destroy units in the cluster. The following table lists the commands provided by `fleetctl`:

Command	Description	Example

`fleetctl list-unit-files`	List all units in the fleet cluster.	`$ fleetctl list-unit-files`
		`UNIT        HASH    DSTATE STATE   TMACHINE`
		`myservice.service d4d81cf launched launched 85c0c595.../172.17.8.102`
		`example.service   e56c91e launched launched 113f16a7.../172.17.8.103`

`fleetctl start`	To start a unit.	`$ fleetctl start myservice.service` `Unit myservice.service launched on d4d81cf.../172.17.8.102`
`fleetctl stop`	To stop a unit.	`$ fleetctl stop myservice.service` `Unit myservice.service stopped on d4d81cf.../172.17.8.102`
`fleetctl load`	To schedule a unit in a cluster without starting the unit. This unit will be in an inactive state.	`$ fleetctl load example.service` `Unit example.service loaded on 133f19a7.../172.17.8.103`
`fleetctl unload`	To unschedule a unit in a cluster. This unit will be visible in `fleetctl list-unit-files` but will not have any state.	`$ fleetctl load example.service`
`fleetctl submit`	To bring the units into the cluster. This unit will be visible in `fleetctl list-unit-files` but will not have any state.	`fleetctl submit example.service`
`fleetctl destroy`	The destroy command stops the unit and removes the unit file from the cluster.	`fleetctl destroy example.service`

Command	Description	Example

`fleetctl status`	To get the status of the unit. This command invokes the `systemctl` command on the machine running a given unit over SSH.	`$ fleetctl status example.service`
		`example.service - Hello World`
		`    Loaded: loaded (/run/systemd/`
		`system/example.service; enabled-`
		`runtime)`
		`    Active: active (running) since`
		`Mon 2015-09-21 23:20:23 UTC; 1h`
		`49min ago`
		`  Main PID: 6972 (bash)`
		`    CGroup: /system.slice/`
		`example.1.service`
		`            ├─ 6973 /bin/bash -c`
		`while true; do echo "Hello, world";`
		`sleep 1; done`
		`            └─20381 sleep 1`

The `fleetctl` syntax looks similar to `systemctl`, which is the management interface for `systemd`.

Standard (local) and global units

Global units are units that are scheduled to run on all the members. Standard or local units are units that are scheduled to run only on some machines. In case of failures, these units are switched to another member in the cluster fit to run those units.

Unit file options for fleet

Unit file format is the same as the file format for `systemd`. fleet extends the configuration by adding another section, `X-Fleet`. This section is used by fleet to schedule the units on a specific member based on the constraints specified. Some of the important parameters of the `X-Fleet` section are:

- `MachineID`: This specifies the machine on which the unit has to be executed. Machine ID can be obtained from the `/etc/machine-id` file, or through the `fleetctl list-machines -l` command. This option is to be used with discretion as it defies the purpose of fleet, allowing a unit to be targeted specifically on the machine.

- `MachineOf`: This instructs fleet to execute the unit on which the specified unit is running. This option can be used to group units running on a member.

- **MachineMetadata**: This instructs fleet to execute the units on the member matching the specified metadata. If more than one metadata is provided, all metadata should match. To match any of the metadata the parameter can include multiple times. Metadata is provided for the member in the cloud-config fleet configuration.

- **Conflicts**: This instructs fleet not to execute the unit on the specified unit that is running.

- **Global**: If this is set to true, the unit is scheduled to be executed on all the members. Additionally, if MachineMetadata is configured, they run only on members having matching metadata. Any other options, if provided, make the unit configuration invalid.

Instantiating the service unit in the cluster

We have seen what CoreOS clustering is, how to form a cluster, and tools like fleet and fleetctl. Now, let us see how a service unit can be started in one of the nodes in the cluster using fleet. As mentioned already, fleetctl is the command-line utility provided by the CoreOS distribution to perform various operations, such as start the service, stop the service, and so on in a cluster. Like systemctl, fleetctl also requires a service file to perform these operations. Let us see a sample service file and using the service file, how fleet starts the service in the cluster:

```
[Unit]
Description=Example
After=docker.service
Requires=docker.service

[Service]
TimeoutStartSec=0
ExecStartPre=-/usr/bin/docker kill busybox1
ExecStartPre=-/usr/bin/docker rm busybox1
ExecStartPre=/usr/bin/docker pull busybox
ExecStart=/usr/bin/docker run --name busybox1 busybox /bin/sh -c
"while true; do echo Hello World; sleep 1; done"
ExecStop=/usr/bin/docker stop busybox1
```

Save the preceding file as `example.service` on the CoreOS machine. Now, execute the following command to start the service in the cluster:

```
$ fleetctl start example.service
```

```
$ fleetctl list-units
UNIT                  MACHINE              ACTIVE    SUB
example.service       d0ef0562.../10.0.0.3  active    running
```

```
$ fleetctl list-machines
MACHINE                                    IP         METADATA
159b2900-7f06-5d43-92da-daeeabb90d5a       10.0.0.1   -
50a69aa6-518d-4d81-ad3d-bfc4d146e996       10.0.0.2   -
d0ef0562-6a6f-1d80-b7e6-46e996bfc4d1       10.0.0.3   -
```

One of the major requirements for running a service is to provide high availability. To provide a high-availability service, we may need to run multiple instances of the same service. These different instances should be running on different nodes. To provide high availability for a unit/service, we should make sure that the different instances of the service are running on different nodes in the cluster. This can be achieved in CoreOS by using the `conflicts` attribute. Let us have a look at the service file for these two instances of the service, say, the service as `redis.service`:

```
[Unit]
Description=My redis Frontend
After=docker.service
Requires=docker.service

[Service]
TimeoutStartSec=0
ExecStartPre=-/usr/bin/docker kill redis
ExecStartPre=-/usr/bin/docker rm redis
ExecStartPre docker pull dockerfile/redis
ExecStart docker run -d --name redis -p 6379:6379 dockerfile/redis
ExecStop=/usr/bin/docker stop redis

[X-Fleet]
Conflicts=redis@*.service
```

Save this content as `redis@1.service` and `redis@2.service`. The conflicts attributes in the service file informs fleet not to start these two services in the same node:

```
$ fleetctl start redis@1
$ fleetctl start redis@2
$ fleetctl list-units
UNIT                MACHINE              ACTIVE    SUB
redis@1.service  5a2686a6.../10.0.0.2   active    running
redis@2.service  259b18ff.../10.0.0.1   active    running
```

Recovering from node failure

CoreOS provides an inherent mechanism to reschedule the units from one node to another node when there is a node failure or machine failure. All the nodes in the cluster send a heartbeat message to the fleet leader. When the heartbeat messages are not received from a particular node, all the units running on that node are marked to be rescheduled in different nodes. The fleet engine identifies the qualified node and starts the units in the qualified node.

Summary

In this chapter, we learned about CoreOS clusters and how members join a cluster using cluster discovery. We got ourselves familiar with the init system used to start the units in most of the Linux systems and how CoreOS extends it to a multi-member cluster using the fleet service. We learned about starting and stopping a service on a member using fleet.

In the next chapter, we will understand more about the constraints on the service, which helps fleet select the member suitable for it to run.

4
Managing Services with User-Defined Constraints

This chapter takes the CoreOS cluster to the next level by putting constraints on the services so that they run on the required members.

This chapter covers the following topics:

- Pre-defined constraints using metadata
- Service-level affinity/anti-affinity
- Node-level affinity
- High availability

Introduction to service constraints

Not all cluster members run all the services in a deployment. Some may run the services running business logic, some may run management software, and some may run logging or auditing software, and so on. Hence, it's imperative that cluster management software provides mechanisms to control service deployment so they run only on the members satisfying their properties. We will study the mechanisms provided by CoreOS to control the deployment.

CoreOS uses the `fleet` service to schedule the services on the members with constraints. Unit file configuration options help to target a service on a particular member or members meeting configured properties. In due course, we will also learn to integrate the `fleet` service into the `cloud-config` file and auto start a custom service inside a `docker` container.

Predefined constraints using metadata

This mechanism enables a service to be runn on a machine having matching metadata configured in the `metadata` parameter of the `coreos.fleet` section. Metadata can be used to describe a member properties such as disk type, region, platform, and special member property like exposed public IPs and so on. Since it is provided as a multiple key-value pair, the flexibility it provides is immense for defining a member.

The metadata can then also be used to associate services to be run on those members. For instance, we can say that a particular service is supposed to run on members that are running in a particular region and/or having a particular disk type and/or having a particular member type (bare metal, cloud, and so on) and/or having a particular provider (machine vendor, cloud provider, and so on).

In our example, we will create three members, each having their own metadata, and then bind the service to run on a metadata matching its property. The following is the setup:

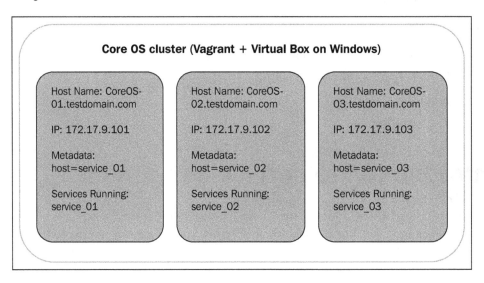

The following is the `cloud-config` file used to create the cluster with services running on their designated members:

```
#cloud-config
write_files:
 - path: /home/core/example_01.service
   owner: core:core
   permissions: 420
   content: |
     [Unit]
     Description=Example
     After=docker.service
     Requires=docker.service

     [X-Fleet]
     MachineMetadata=host=service_01

     [Service]
     TimeoutStartSec=0
     ExecStartPre=-/usr/bin/docker kill sampleserv_01
     ExecStartPre=-/usr/bin/docker rm sampleserv_01
     ExecStartPre=/usr/bin/docker pull busybox
     ExecStart=/usr/bin/docker run --name sampleserv_01 busybox
     /bin/sh -c "while true; do echo Test Service; sleep 300;
     done"
     ExecStop=/usr/bin/docker stop sampleserv_01

 - path: /home/core/example_02.service
   owner: core:core
   permissions: 420
   content: |
     [Unit]
     Description=Example
     After=docker.service
     Requires=docker.service

     [X-Fleet]
     MachineMetadata=host=service_02

     [Service]
     TimeoutStartSec=0
     ExecStartPre=-/usr/bin/docker kill sampleserv_02
     ExecStartPre=-/usr/bin/docker rm sampleserv_02
     ExecStartPre=/usr/bin/docker pull busybox
```

```
    ExecStart=/usr/bin/docker run --name sampleserv_02 busybox
    /bin/sh -c "while true; do echo Test Service; sleep 300;
    done"
    ExecStop=/usr/bin/docker stop sampleserv_02

  - path: /home/core/example_03.service
    owner: core:core
    permissions: 420
    content: |
      [Unit]
      Description=Example
      After=docker.service
      Requires=docker.service

      [X-Fleet]
      MachineMetadata=host=service_03

      [Service]
      TimeoutStartSec=0
      ExecStartPre=-/usr/bin/docker kill sampleserv_03
      ExecStartPre=-/usr/bin/docker rm sampleserv_03
      ExecStartPre=/usr/bin/docker pull busybox
      ExecStart=/usr/bin/docker run --name sampleserv_03 busybox
      /bin/sh -c "while true; do echo Test Service; sleep 300;
      done"
      ExecStop=/usr/bin/docker stop sampleserv_03

coreos:
  etcd2:
    name: core-03
    advertise-client-urls: http://$public_ipv4:2379
    initial-advertise-peer-urls: http://$private_ipv4:2380
    listen-client-urls: http://0.0.0.0:2379,http://0.0.0.0:4001
    listen-peer-urls:
    http://$private_ipv4:2380,http://$private_ipv4:7001
    initial-cluster-token: coreOS-static
    initial-cluster: core-01=http://172.17.8.101:2380,core-
    02=http://172.17.8.102:2380,core-03=http://172.17.8.103:2380
  fleet:
    public-ip: $public_ipv4
    metadata: host=service_01

  units:
  - name: etcd2.service
    command: start
```

```
  enable: true
- name: fleet.service
  command: start
  enable: true
- name: example_fleet_01.service
  command: start
  content: |
    [Service]
    Type=oneshot
    ExecStartPre=/bin/sh -c "sleep 10"
    ExecStart=/usr/bin/fleetctl start
    /home/core/example_01.service
- name: example_fleet_02.service
  command: start
  content: |
    [Service]
    Type=oneshot
    ExecStartPre=/bin/sh -c "sleep 10"
    ExecStart=/usr/bin/fleetctl start
    /home/core/example_02.service
- name: example_fleet_03.service
  command: start
  content: |
    [Service]
    Type=oneshot
    ExecStartPre=/bin/sh -c "sleep 10"
    ExecStart=/usr/bin/fleetctl start
    /home/core/example_03.service
```

The `write_files` section is added to generate the unit files for `fleet`. Three unit files are created; each service would be running only one of the members. Each unit file has the `X-Fleet` section adding a constraint that it should only run on a machine having specific metadata.

The `fleet` section updated to start `fleet` and specify the IP address used to contact the `etcd2` service. Additionally, the metadata parameter is added to specify the metadata for the member. Instrumentation is required to generate separate metadata for each of the members. `Vagrantfile` for the static cluster in *Chapter 3, Creating Your Coreos Cluster and Managing the Cluster*, is used as the base file and the highlighted instrumentation is done to modify metadata for each of the members.

```
        . . .
        if File.exist?(CLOUD_CONFIG_PATH)
          user_data_specific = "#{CLOUD_CONFIG_PATH}-#{i}"
          require 'yaml'
```

```
        data = YAML.load(IO.readlines('user-data')[1..-1].join)
        if data['coreos'].key? 'etcd2'
          data['coreos']['etcd2']['name'] = vm_name
        end
        if data['coreos'].key? 'fleet'
          data['coreos']['fleet']['metadata'] =
          "host=service_%02d" % [i]
        end
        yaml = YAML.dump(data)
        File.open(user_data_specific, 'w') { |file|
        file.write("#cloud-config\n\n#{yaml}") }
        config.vm.provision :file, :source => user_data_specific,
        :destination => "/tmp/vagrantfile-user-data"
        config.vm.provision :shell, :inline => "mv
        /tmp/vagrantfile-user-data /var/lib/coreos-vagrant/",
        :privileged => true
      end
  ...
```

The units section is updated to start the `fleet` service and wrapper `oneshot` service to invoke `fleetctl` upon startup. `Fleetctl` then manages the service. The following is the sequence of events:

- Unit files for the services /home/core/example_01.`service`, /home/core/
  example_02.`service` and /home/core/example_03.`service` are created at
  the time of boot-up. Note that `write_files` is kept before the `coreos` section
  so that the files are created before services are started.

- Services are started by `systemd` running on each member. A sleep of
  ten seconds is added in the `oneshot` services example_01.`service`,
  example_01.`service`, and example_01.`service` to allow initialization of
  `etcd2` and the `fleetd` service before the job is submitted using `fleetctl`.

- `Fleetd` then coordinates and schedules the services on respective members.

Boot the cluster using `Vagrant up`. Upon successful boot-up, we can see the
members in the cluster and the services running on the members. Note that
example_01.`service` is started on `member 01` having the metadata `service_01`,
example_02.`service` is started on `member 01` having the metadata `service_02`,
and so on:

```
vagrant ssh core-01

fleetctl list-units
UNIT                    MACHINE                         ACTIVE  SUB
```

```
example_01.service       375bde8b.../172.17.8.101          active   running
example_02.service       2b6184e0.../172.17.8.102          active   running
example_03.service       e59919cc.../172.17.8.103          active   running
fleetctl list-machines
MACHINE          IP              METADATA
2b6184e0...      172.17.8.102    host=service_02
375bde8b...      172.17.8.101    host=service_01
e59919cc...      172.17.8.103    host=service_03
```

Now, let's modify the `cloud-config` file to create another deployment where one instance of `example.service` is running on every member along with respective services on member 2 and member 3 as the previous example.

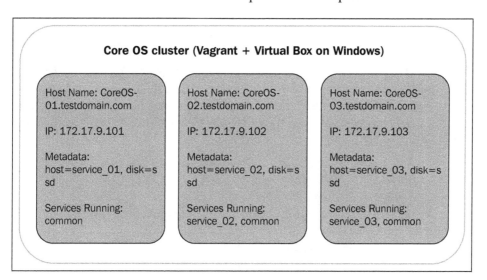

We will now go through the modifications that are required in the `cloud-config` file prepared earlier.

The unit files for `fleetctl` were modified for the first service to create a template unit. A template file helps the creation of multiple units from a single configuration file. While adding a unit, `Fleet/systemd` looks for the configuration file with an exact name match. If such a file is not found, a filename with the same name the @ character is used. For example, to add the unit `common@1` file, `common@.service` will be used.

```
#cloud-config
write_files:
  - path: /home/core/common@.service
  ...
```

Additional constraints were added to the section X-Fleet. MachineMetaData was changed to use the disk as ssd. Metadata disk=ssd is also added to all the members using Vagrantfile instrumentation. This makes the service fit for running on all members. The additional constraint Conflicts is added so that only one instance of this service runs on a machine. This constraint means that if a service is already running on the member, other instances of the service can't be scheduled on the same machine. Note how the service name is provided with a wildcard to match any of the instance numbers.

```
. . .
    [X-Fleet]
    MachineMetadata=disk=ssd
    Conflicts=common@*.service
. . .
```

The service section of the unit file is updated to be capable of spawning a service for any instance. To refer to the instance string from within the configuration file, we can use %i specifier. %i gets replaced with the instance number provided during start. This feature was not required to be used in the example but is worth a mention.

```
. . .

    [Service]
    TimeoutStartSec=0
    ExecStartPre=-/usr/bin/docker kill busybox
    ExecStartPre=-/usr/bin/docker rm busybox
    ExecStartPre=/usr/bin/docker pull busybox
    ExecStart=/usr/bin/docker run --name busybox /bin/sh -c
    "while true; do echo Test Service; sleep 300; done"
    ExecStop=/usr/bin/docker stop busybox
. . .
```

The wrapper service to invoke fleetctl is also updated to start three instances of service:

```
. . .
  - name: example_fleet1.service
    command: start
    content: |
      [Service]
      Type=oneshot
      ExecStartPre=/bin/sh -c "sleep 10"
      ExecStart=/usr/bin/fleetctl start
      /home/core/common@1.service
  - name: example_fleet2.service
. . .
```

```
        ExecStart=/usr/bin/fleetctl start
        /home/core/common@2.service
  - name: example_fleet3.service
...

        ExecStart=/usr/bin/fleetctl start
        /home/core/common@3.service
  - name: example_fleet_02.service
...
```

`Vagrantfile` was modified with the following instrumentation to add the metadata `disk=ssd` to all the members:

```
...
        if data['coreos'].key? 'fleet'
          data['coreos']['fleet']['metadata'] =
          "host=service_%02d,disk=ssd" % [i]
        end
...
```

Boot the cluster using `Vagrant up`. Upon successful boot-up, we can see the members in the cluster and the services running on the members. Note that `common@.service` is running on all the members, whereas `example_02.service` and `example_03.service` are only instantiated on respective members.

```
vagrant ssh core-01
```

```
fleetctl list-units
```

UNIT	MACHINE	ACTIVE	SUB
common@1.service	344d088c.../172.17.8.102	active	running
common@2.service	a5a4a7e5.../172.17.8.101	active	running
common@3.service	200545ed.../172.17.8.103	active	running
example_02.service	344d088c.../172.17.8.102	active	running
example_03.service	200545ed.../172.17.8.103	active	running

```
fleetctl list-machines
```

MACHINE	IP	METADATA
200545ed...	172.17.8.103	disk=ssd,host=service_03
344d088c...	172.17.8.102	disk=ssd,host=service_02
a5a4a7e5...	172.17.8.101	disk=ssd,host=service_01

In this example, we also touched upon constraints based on running services on the machine. We will discuss it further in the next section.

Service level affinity/anti-affinity

This mechanism enables clubbing services together, to be run on the same member or vice versa; that is, making sure that if a particular service is running on the member, the current service is not to be scheduled on that machine.

In the second example for predefined constraints using metadata, we added a constraint, `Conflicts`, so that only one instance of service is started on a member. Hence, the constraint was added for the self-service name. This can also be added for another service. This ensures that two services don't co-exist in a member. To understand this, we will modify the example slightly so that `common@.service` doesn't run along with `example_02.service`.

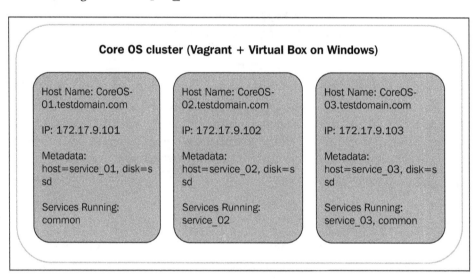

Another `Conflicts` parameter is added for `example_02.server` in the unit configuration file of `common@.service`. Also, the `units` section of `coreos` is modified to add an entry for `example_fleet_02.service` before `example_fleet1.service`.

```
. . .
    [X-Fleet]
    MachineMetadata=disk=ssd
    Conflicts=common@*.service
    Conflicts=example_02.service
. . .
```

Boot the cluster using `Vagrant up`. Upon successful boot-up, we can see the members in the cluster and the services running on the members. Note that `common@.service` is running on all the members except on the member where `example_02.service` is running.

```
vagrant ssh core-01
```

```
fleetctl list-units
```

UNIT	MACHINE	ACTIVE	SUB
common@1.service	60b21422.../172.17.8.101	active	running
common@2.service	c8009511.../172.17.8.103	active	running
example_02.service	103f8f5a.../172.17.8.102	active	running
example_03.service	c8009511.../172.17.8.103	active	running

```
fleetctl list-machines
```

MACHINE	IP	METADATA
103f8f5a...	172.17.8.102	disk=ssd,host=service_02
60b21422...	172.17.8.101	disk=ssd,host=service_01
c8009511...	172.17.8.103	disk=ssd,host=service_03

Now let's discuss a reverse use case: we want a particular service to run on a member with another service. We will run the common service only where `example_02.service` is running.

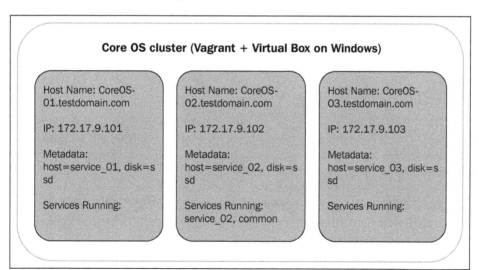

The X-Fleet section is updated with the new parameter MachineOf. This ensures that common@.service only runs along with example_02.service.

```
. . .
        [X-Fleet]
        MachineOf=example_02.service
. . .
```

Boot the cluster using Vagrant up. Upon successful boot-up, we can see the members in the cluster and the services running on the members. Note that common@1.service is running only on the member where example_02.service is running.

```
vagrant ssh core-01
```

```
core@core-01 ~ $ fleetctl list-units
UNIT                     MACHINE                        ACTIVE   SUB
common@1.service         d119aafa.../172.17.8.102       active   running
example_02.service       d119aafa.../172.17.8.102       active   running
example_03.service       6f3da0a4.../172.17.8.103       active   running
core@core-01 ~ $
core@core-01 ~ $
core@core-01 ~ $ fleetctl list-machines
MACHINE          IP              METADATA
6f3da0a4...      172.17.8.103    disk=ssd,host=service_03
c88e05ba...      172.17.8.101    disk=ssd,host=service_01
d119aafa...      172.17.8.102    disk=ssd,host=service_02
```

Node-level affinity

This mechanism uses the systemd generated machine ID to schedule the services. Upon member installation, systemd generates a machine ID that is the same across subsequent system boots. Node-level affinity ensures the user targets a service onto a member and nowhere else. When thinking about clusters where it's more flexible to schedule a service based on member properties rather than on member identifiers, this mechanism has limited use. Typical use cases can be running a service to collect specific data from a machine, or for testing a service where a new service can be scheduled on a test member for observing the behavior.

The following is the `cloud-config` file used to create the cluster. This file also creates a service unit file in the home directory that will be used by fleet to start the service.

```
#cloud-config
write_files:
  - path: /home/core/example_test.service
    owner: core:core
    permissions: 420
    content: |
      [Unit]
      Description=Example
      After=docker.service
      Requires=docker.service

      [X-Fleet]
      MachineID=dummy

      [Service]
      TimeoutStartSec=0
      ExecStartPre=-/usr/bin/docker kill sampleserv_test
      ExecStartPre=-/usr/bin/docker rm sampleserv_test
      ExecStartPre=/usr/bin/docker pull busybox
      ExecStart=/usr/bin/docker run --name sampleserv_test busybox
      /bin/sh -c "while true; do echo Test Service; sleep 300;
      done"
      ExecStop=/usr/bin/docker stop sampleserv_test

  ...

  units:
  - name: etcd2.service
    command: start
    enable: true
  - name: fleet.service
    command: start
    enable: true
```

This `cloud-config` file serves two main purpose: starting `fleetd` services and creating the service file `/home/core/example_test.service`.

We will now find the machine IDs of members in the cluster:

```
vagrant ssh core-01
```

```
core@core-01 ~ $ fleetctl list-machines -l
MACHINE                            IP              METADATA
41b7574b33b0462c8e311ded39302a19   172.17.8.101    host=service_01
7e481484a52945d3ad369f68d2e46a77   172.17.8.103    host=service_03
f70fc5f45cdc49f99fc47757f6fe5ae6   172.17.8.102    host=service_02
```

Modify the service file so that the service is instantiated on the machine ID `f70fc5f45cdc49f99fc47757f6fe5ae6`. This can be any machine ID of your choice. We are not able to automate using Vagrant as machine IDs are not known to us earlier.

```
core@core-01 ~ $ cat example_test.service
...


[X-Fleet]
MachineID=f70fc5f45cdc49f99fc47757f6fe5ae6


...
```

Launch the service and check that it's running on the desired machine:

```
core@core-01 ~ $ /usr/bin/fleetctl start /home/core/example_test.service
Unit example_test.service launched on f70fc5f4.../172.17.8.102
core@core-01 ~ $ fleetctl list-units
UNIT                      MACHINE                      ACTIVE
SUB
example_test.service      f70fc5f4.../172.17.8.102        active
running
```

High availability

There are two key principles in designing a highly available system. One is to avoid single point of failure; that is, the complete system should not fail when a fault occurs. For example, there should not be a dependency on a single process, interface, and so on. The second principle is how quickly the system can recover in case of failure so that downtime is short.

`Fleetd` helps design a highly available system by allowing the configuration of multiple instances of the service on different members and not multiple instances on the same member. This means that the failure of a single member doesn't bring down the complete service, but it can still perform the function it's supposed to do with reduced capacity until a recovery happens. Once the member is recovered or another member is started by the orchestration application detecting member failure, fleet will reschedule the service on the new member automatically.

Summary

In this chapter, we understood service constraints which help to deploy services on suitable members.

In the next chapter, we will understand more about discovering services running in the CoreOS cluster.

5
Discovering Services Running in a Cluster

When there are large numbers of members in a deployment, it's very important for the system to have easy manageability with the least human intervention possible. Human interventions tend to have human errors associated with them, making the system unstable. Imagine a scenario where there is a load balancer, which distributes HTTP traffic to multiple servers. If any servers go down or come up, it's very important that the load balancer knows about a node or service addition or deletion automatically without manual intervention, else it will be a nightmare managing such deployments. Service discovery ensures that the load balancer is aware of the currently active instances of services; based on this, it can take routing decisions.

This chapter explains the need and mechanism for the discovery of services running on a cluster.

This chapter covers the following topics:

- Introduction and necessity of service discovery
- Mechanism for discovery of services.

Introduction and necessity of service discovery

In a CoreOS environment, all of the user applications will be deployed as services inside a container. For most of these, user applications need to work coherently and hence, a mechanism is needed to discover these services and service parameters. Service discovery via etcd provides a way to publish the services and the required parameters with a service to other services in the system. The service discovery mechanism is not only useful for service parameter discovery but also involves the detection of the change of state of a member (the addition of a new member or the removal of a member running a service or a member going down), the state of the service (the service providing an application comes up or goes down), and service parameters (like the IP and port on which the service is provided, database connection end points, and so on). It is a requirement that the service information is available across all members at all times, which means that the mechanism for service discovery should be replicated and made available through multiple members to avoid single point of failure.

Mechanism for service discovery

Features provided by the CoreOS services `etcd` and `fleetd` can be used to discover services. The following figure explains the typical mechanism used for service discovery:

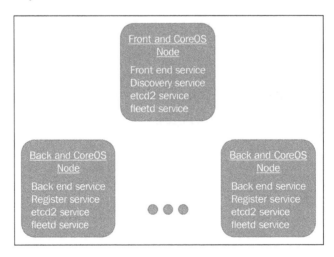

In the previous chapters, we have seen how etcd and fleetd can be used to discover the member nodes in a cluster. The etcd service is not limited for node discovery. It can be used to discover or publish information related to applications or services. The subsequent sections in this chapter cover how to publish and discover service-related information using etcd.

There are two kinds of member nodes in the cluster: frontend service nodes and backend service nodes.

- The frontend service handles all service requests and routes the request to the backend service for actual processing. This is the simplified but typical architecture for any high-capacity system. In the frontend service nodes, the following services will be running:
  - Discovery service
  - etcd service
  - fleetd service
  - Frontend or route service

- Backend service nodes are responsible for running the services that are being scheduled or routed by the frontend service nodes. In the backend service nodes, the following services will be running:
  - Register service: If simple discovery is required, this can be included in the backend service unit file as ExeStartPost
  - etcd service
  - fleetd service
  - Backend or actual service

The fleetd and etcd services are already discussed in detail in previous chapters. The Register service running in backend nodes updates the service information in the etcd key-value store, which will be published to the discovery service. The discovery services running in the frontend nodes are used to discover the backend member service information using etcd key-value store information.

Let's understand the complete flow of discovery step by step:

- The `Frontend` member is started. The fleetd service kicks in and schedules the `Frontend` and `Discovery` service . Service level affinity is used to ensure that both of them run together on a member.

- The `Discovery` service uses the `etcd` key-value store feature to look for backend member information. It also sets up a watch so that it comes to know of any changes in the service discovery information. We will learn about reading, writing, and setting up a watch on etcd later in this chapter. Since backend members are not started, no service information is available yet, so the discovery service is in wait mode looking for any updates in service information.

- One of the `backend` member is started. The `fleetd` service again kicks in and schedules the `Backend` and `Register` service. Here, also, service level affinity is used to ensure that both of them run together on a member. The Register service updates the service information in the `etcd` key-value store. This service information is useful for the frontend member. Service information can be endpoint information like IP and port, service type, or any other metadata necessary for the frontend to take an informed decision on scheduling the request. It's also important that a time to live is set on such data and the data is being periodically rewritten on etcd. Setting time to live on data ensures that service data also gets removed when service terminates.

- Since the `Discovery` service on the frontend member has set up a watch on etcd, it comes to know about new service instance additions. It then updates the frontend service that adds the service instance. Based on the information available, the frontend service can start scheduling the incoming request to the service instance.

- Once other members are started, service discovery keeps on happening as explained in the previous step and the frontend service becomes aware of more and more service instances for the scheduling request.

- Now, assume one of the members went down. The service information gets erased from `etcd` after the time to live if they are not updated again. The same will happen when the member is up and running but the backend service goes down and is not able to come up again. In this scenario, `fleetd` will bring down the Register service also, since they are bound together. If they don't come up further on the member, the service parameter will again expire on `etcd` after time to live.

- Parameter deletion is again detected by the `Discovery` service and the information passed to the `Frontend` service. The `Frontend` service now knows that there is one less service instance to work on.

Note that this is only a conceptual representation of the whole process. There is no restriction that your frontend application and discovery services should be two separate applications or services. There is a possibility that your frontend application could also contain the discovery services. When you use a third party or readymade frontend application like HAProxy, then you may need to write a thin discovery service or you can also use confd, another readymade application for discovery. Similarly, the backend service and register service can be fused together or you can use another readymade application, forest, to directly update etcd without writing a register service.

Operations of etcd

etcd provides the following three operations for manipulating the key-value store:

- etcd write
- etcd read
- etcd watch

There are two main interfaces provided by CoreOS to perform the preceding etcd operations:

- etcdctl
- REST-based interface. cURL can be used to invoke REST APIs.

Operations using etcdctl

etcdctl is a command-line client of etcd. Using etcdctl, you can read, write, and watch the key-value store of etcd. etcdctl can be used as a standalone tool for configuring the key-value store or can also be used in scripts. etcdctl sends the request message to the etcd service and waits for the response from etcd. etcdctl can return any one of the following return codes:

Return value	Semantics
0	Success
1	Malformed etcdctl arguments
2	Failed to connect to host
3	Failed to auth (client cert rejected, ca validation failure, and so on)
4	400 error from etcd
5	500 error from etcd

etcd write using etcdctl

The etcd write service will be used by the backend nodes to publish the service information using the key-value data store to the frontend services.

The following write operations are possible using `etcdctl`. The following table lists the command options provided by `etcdctl` with syntax and examples:

Operations	Command syntax	Example
Setting value for a key	`etcdctl set <key> <value>`	`$ etcdctl set /foo/bar "foo bar"`
Setting value for a key with expiry in seconds	`etcdctl set <key> <value> -ttl`	`$ etcdctl set /foo/bar "foo bar" -ttl 10`
Conditionally setting value for a key based on the previous value	`etcdctl set /<key> <old-value> --swap-with-value <new-value>`	`$ etcdctl set /foo/bar "foo bar" --swap-with-value "bar foo"`
Creating a new key	`etcdctl mk <key> <value>`	`$ etcdctl mk /foo/bar "foo bar"`
Creating a new directory	`etcdctl mkdir <dir>`	`$ etcdctl mkdir /foo/bar`
Updating value for a key	`etcdctl update <key> <value>`	`$ etcdctl set /foo/bar "bar foo"`
Deleting a key	`etcdctl rm <key>`	`$ etcdctl rm /foo/bar`
Deleting a key and all its child key recursively	`etcdctl rm <key> --recursive`	`$ etcdctl rm /foo/bar -recursive`
Conditionally deleting a key	`etcdctl rm <key> --with-value <value>`	`$ etcdctl rm /foo/bar --with-value "foo bar"`
Deleting a directory	`etcdctl rmdir <dir>`	`$ etcdctl rmdir /foo/bar`

etcd read using etcdctl

The `etcd read` service will be used by the frontend nodes to discover the service information using the key-value data store.

The following read operations are possible using `etcdctl`. The following table lists the command options provided by `etcdctl` with syntax and examples:

Operations	Command syntax	Example
Retrieving a key-value	`etcdctl get <key>`	`$ etcdctl get /foo/bar` `foo bar`
Retrieving a key-value with additional metadata	`etcdctl -o extended get <key>`	`$ etcdctl -o extended get /foo/bar` Key: /foo/bar Modified-Index: 72 TTL: 0 Etcd-Index: 72 Raft-Index: 5611 Raft-Term: 1 foo bar
Creating a new key	`etcdctl mk <key> <value>`	`$ etcdctl mk /foo/bar` `"foo bar"`
Listing the directory	`etcdctl ls`	`$ etcdctl ls` `/foo`

Listing the directory recursively	`etcdctl ls - recursive`	`$ etcdctl ls`
		`--recursive`
		`/foo`
		`/foo/bar`

With our `testservices` example, the following command is used to read the parameters using `etcdctl`. Note that we are using the `ls` command here to get the list of services and then querying on a specific service instance.

```
etcdctl ls /testservice/backend/1
/testservice/backend/1
/testservice/backend/2

etcdctl get /testservice/backend/2
172.17.8.102:55555
```

etcd watch using etcdctl

The `etcd watch` service will be used by the frontend nodes to monitor or watch for any change in the key-value data store.

The following watch operations are possible using `etcdctl`. The following table lists the command options provided by `etcdctl` with syntax and examples:

Operations	Command syntax	Example
Watching for any change in the key-value.	`etcdctl watch <key>`	`$ etcdctl watch /foo/bar`
Continuously watching any change in the key-value. In this case, etcdctl hangs forever until *Ctrl + C* and it prints the value when there is a change in the key-value.	`etcdctl watch <key> --forever`	`$ etcdctl watch /foo/bar --forever` `foo bar`
Continuously watching any change in the key-value and executes a program when there is a change in the key-value.	`etcdctl exec-watch <key> --sh -c program to execute`	`$ etcdctl exec-watch -- sh -c env	grep ETCD`

Example of etcd using etcdctl

Until now, we have seen how a service parameter can be published and discovered in theoretical fashion. Now it's time for some practical work. Let's start off by getting ourselves familiar with the etcd key-value store features used for discovery and how to use them with an example of a service called `testservices`, which publishes the IP address and port number on which this service is running.

Here, `testservices` is the directory where all the new service information is added. IP is the IP of the member and `5555` is the port (chosen for this example) on which a service is running.

The following is the command to write the IP address and port on which a service is added with the key as IP:

```
etcdctl set /testservices/ip '172.17.8.101:55555' -ttl 30
```

An optional parameter, `-ttl 30`, is added to set the lifetime for the key as 30 seconds.

In our example, we have chosen to show how to write the IP address and port number key to the key-store. Please note that there are various ways to learn about the IP address on which a service is running programmatically. The environment variables COREOS_PRIVATE_IPV4 and COREOS_PUBLIC_IPV4 can be used or the ipconfig command can be used to find out the IP address assigned for the member.

To get the parameters published by testservices, the following command should be used:

```
etcdctl get /testservices/ip 172.17.8.101:55555
```

To watch these parameters the following command should be used:

```
etcdctl watch /testservices/ip
```

The following are the commands to write entries that we queried using etcdctl before.

```
etcdctl set /testservices/backend/1 172.17.8.101:55555 -ttl 30
etcdctl set /testservices/backend/2 172.17.8.102:55555 -ttl 30
```

Operations using cURL

cURL, often referred to as curl, is a command-line tool used to transfer data to and from application servers using various protocols. cURL supports a range of protocols including **HTTPS, HTTP, FTPS, FTP, SCP, TFTP, SFTP, DAP, LDAP, DICT, TELNET, IMAP, FILE, POP3, SMTP,** and **RTSP**. It is often used for getting or sending files using URL like syntax. Like etcdctl, curl can also be used as a standalone tool for configuring the key-value store or can also be used in scripts. All the operations that can be done using etcdctl can also be done using curl. curl also provides more operations to manipulate the key-value store. curl sends a request message to the etcd service and waits for the response. The response contains the following parameters/attributes:

- Action: The action field represents the type of curl request sent. The action can take the value as get, set, create, delete, update, expire, watch, and so on.

- Node: The node field represents the directories of the key-value store. It consists of key, value, createIndex, and modifiedIndex.

    ○ The key field represents the key of the key-value store.

    ○ The value field represents the value of the key-value store.

- ○ Every node has a field called index, which will be incremented for each change to etcd. The createdIndex field is filled with this index.

- ○ modifiedIndex also represents the index of the node. However, this represents the number of operations that are applied over this node, which changes the value of this key-value store.

A sample output of a curl set command is shown as follows:

```
curl -L http://127.0.0.1:4001/v2/keys/foo/bar -XPUT -d value="foo bar"

{
    "action": "set",
    "node": {
        "createdIndex": 2,
        "key": "/foo/bar",
        "modifiedIndex": 2,
        "value": "foo bar"
    }
}
```

etcd read using curl

The following read operations are possible using curl. The following table lists the command options provided by curl with syntax and examples:

Operations	Command syntax	Example

Retrieving a key-value	curl -L <URL>	curl -L http://127.0.0.1:4001/ v2/keys/foo/bar
		
		{
		  "action": "get",
		  "node": {
		    "createdIndex": 2,
		    "key": "/foo/bar",
		    "modifiedIndex": 2,
		    "value": "foo bar"
		  }
		}

Operations	Command syntax	Example

Retrieving a key-value recursively	`curl -L <URL> ? ?recursive=true&sorted=true`	`curl -L 'http://127.0.0.1:4001/ v2/keys/foo/ bar?recursive=true&sorted=true'`
		
		{
		  "action": "get",
		  "node": {
		    "createdIndex": 2,
		    "key": "/foo/bar",
		    "modifiedIndex": 2,
		    "value": "foo bar"
		  }
		}

etcd write using curl

The following write operations are possible using `curl`. The following table lists the command options provided by curl with syntax and examples:

Operations	Command syntax	Example

Setting value for a key	`curl -L <URL> -XPUT -d value=<value>`	`curl -L http://127.0.0.1:4001/ v2/keys/foo/bar -XPUT -d value="foo bar"`
		
		{
		  "action": "set",
		  "node": {
		    "createdIndex": 2,
		    "key": "/foo/bar",
		    "modifiedIndex": 2,
		    "value": "foo bar "
		  }
		}

Operations	Command syntax	Example

Setting value for a key with expiry in seconds	`curl -L <URL> -XPUT -d value=<value> -d ttl=<value>`	`curl -L http://127.0.0.1:4001/ v2/keys/foo/bar -XPUT -d value="foo bar" -d ttl=5`
		
		{
		  "action": "set",
		  "node": {
		    "createdIndex": 2,
		    "expiration": "2015-12-04T12:11:11.824823581-08:00",
		    "key": "/foo/bar",
		    "modifiedIndex": 2,
		    "ttl": 5,
		    "value": "foo bar"
		  }
		}

Updating value for a key	`curl -L <URL> -XPUT -d value=<value>`	`curl -L http://127.0.0.1:4001/ v2/keys/foo/bar -XPUT -d value="foo bar2"`
		{
		  "action": "set",
		  "node": {
		    "createdIndex": 3,
		    "key": "/foo/bar",
		    "modifiedIndex": 3,
		    "value": "foo bar2 "
		  },
		  "prevNode": {
		    "createdIndex": 2,
		    "key": "/foo/bar",
		    "modifiedIndex": 2,
		    "value": "foo bar "
		  }
		}

Operations	Command syntax	Example

Deleting a key	`curl -L <URL> -XDELETE`	`curl -L http://127.0.0.1:4001/ v2/keys/foo/bar -XDELETE`
		
		 {
		   "action": "delete",
		   "node": {
		     "createdIndex": 3,
		     "key": "/foo/bar",
		     "modifiedIndex": 3
		   },
		   "prevNode": {
		     "createdIndex": 2,
		     "key": "/foo/bar",
		     "modifiedIndex": 2,
		     "value": "foo bar "
		   }
		 }

etcd watch using curl

The following watch operations are possible using `curl`. The following table lists the command options provided by curl with syntax and examples:

Operations	Command syntax	Example
Watching for any change in the key-value	`curl -L <URL>?wait=true`	`curl -L http://127.0.0.1:4001/ v2/keys/foo/bar?wait=true`

Example using curl

Let's see how to use curl with our `testservices` that want to publish the IP address and port number in which this service is running.

Here, `testservices` is the directory where all the new service information is added. IP is the IP of the member and `5555` is the port (chosen for this example) on which a service is running.

The following is the command to write the IP address and port on which a service is added with the key as IP:

```
curl -L http://127.0.0.1:4001/v2/keys/testservices/ip -XPUT -d
value="'172.17.8.101:5555"
```

```
{
    "action": "set",
    "node": {
        "createdIndex": 3,
        "key": "/ testservices/ip ",
        "modifiedIndex": 3,
        "value": "'172.17.8.101:5555"
    }
}
```

To get the parameters published by testservices, the following command should be used:

```
curl -L 'http://127.0.0.1:4001/v2/keys/testservices/ip'
```

```
{
    "action": "get",
    "node": {
        "createdIndex": 4,
        "key": "/ testservices/ip ",
        "modifiedIndex": 4,
        "value": "'172.17.8.101:5555"
    }
}
```

To watch these parameters, the following command should be used:

```
curl -L http://127.0.0.1:4001/v2/keys/ testservices/ip'?wait=true
```

HAProxy and service discovery

In this section, we use service discovery to create a web service that has multiple backend nodes with HAProxy frontend and then load balancing the service requests. HAProxy is a commonly used load balancer for TCP and HTTP-based applications.

Let's start by understanding a typical HAProxy configuration. We are not going to cover the HAProxy configuration exhaustively, but will only concentrate on the configurations that are relevant for service discovery:

```
frontend testloadbalancer
    bind *:80
    mode http
    balance roundrobin
    server testserver01 172.17.18.101:80 check
    server testserver02 172.17.18.102:80 check
```

This configuration instructs HAProxy to bind to port 80 and forward HTTP traffic to the servers `172.17.18.10` and `172.17.18.102` in a round robin fashion. When we have information on every backend server, we can configure HAProxy statically and the setup will work. But imagine a scenario where the information on the IP is not available. For example, when IPs are allocated dynamically or the number of nodes keeps increasing as the traffic to the server increases. We can use service discovery to keep HAProxy updated with the addition and deletion of the backend dynamically. We will make ourselves familiar with another tool called confd. We will use confd as a discovery service. confd has the capability of watching the etcd key store, it then prepares a configuration file based on the template and copies the configuration file to the location required by the applications, and invokes a command asking an application to reload the configuration.

confd requires a template application configuration file in the directory /etc/confd/ templates and a confd configuration file in the directory /etc/confd/conf.d.

The following is the configuration file testconfd.toml for confd:

```
[template]
src = "haproxy.cfg.tmpl"
dest = "/etc/haproxy/haproxy.cfg"
keys = [
  "/testservice/backend",
]
reload_cmd = "/usr/sbin/service haproxy reload"
```

This configuration file mentions that the HAProxy template filename is haproxy. cfg.tmpl. The configuration file prepared based on the template file has to be copied to /etc/haproxy/haproxy.cfg. The configuration file also mentions that the etcd key is /testservice/backend. Finally, it invokes the command to reload HAProxy.

The following is how the template file `haproxy.cfg.tmpl` would look for the HAProxy configuration file we have seen before:

```
frontend testloadbalancer
    bind *:80
    mode http
    balance roundrobin
    {{range $serveraddr := . testservice backend}}
    server {{Base $serveraddr.Key}} {{$serveraddr.Value}} check
    {{end}}
```

The range directive loops through etcd keys and prepares the entries for each name. The base directive used is very similar to the base-name utility of Linux. For the etcd keys written in this chapter before, the corresponding entries would be:

```
server 1 172.17.18.101:55555 check
server 2 172.17.18.102:55555 check
```

Now, coming to the backend servers, we can add the command (`etcdctl` or `curl`) to update the system IP address in etcd using `ExeStartPost`. confd would then update the frontend HAProxy with the new configuration as and when backend servers come up.

Summary

In this chapter, we understood discovery services, why it is very important while developing services or applications in a CoreOS environment, how to publish a service and its parameters, and how to watch for changes in the state of the services. We also learned about the two important tools, etcdctl and curl, that are widely used for service discovery, with some examples.

In the next chapter, we will learn how different services running inside a CoreOS cluster can communicate with each other using service chaining mechanisms.

6
Service Chaining and Networking Across Services

This chapter explains the need and mechanism for chaining different services running in a cluster.

This chapter covers the following topics:

- Introduction to and necessity of service chaining
- Introduction to Docker networking
- Service chaining using Flannel/Rudder
- Service chaining using Weave

In the previous chapter, we discussed in detail how the services running in different CoreOS instances can be discovered from other services. Once the services are discovered, one or more services may need to talk to each other. This chapter explains the need and mechanism for chaining different services running in the CoreOS cluster.

Introduction to and necessity of service chaining

As different services in the CoreOS clusters are deployed as a docker/Rackt container, it is inevitable that we will provide a mechanism to communicate between these services. These services may run in the same CoreOS instances of a cluster or they may run across different CoreOS instances in the cluster.

An example is, when a web server is deployed in node1 of a CoreOS cluster and database services are deployed in node2 of the cluster. Here, the database service provides a service to the web server and we can call this a service provider. Using the service discovery mechanisms described in the previous chapter, the web server service may discover the database service and its parameters such as its connection string with IP, port no., and so on. Once this information is discovered, the web server may need to interact with the database service for storing some information persistently or to fetch some information from the persistent storage. In order to do this, it may need to do the following:

- Establish a network connection between each other
- Use the service provided by the service provider

Everything looks fine. But when providing a network connection between the containers, there are some complexities. Let's look into those. Throughout this chapter, we assume that the services in the CoreOS instances are deployed as a docker container.

Each service/docker container in the CoreOS node is assigned an IP address. This IP address can be used by the applications running in the container to talk/communicate with each other. This works well when the services are running in the same CoreOS node. This is because all of the docker instances or services running in the same CoreOS node will be part of the same network, which will be connected by the docker0 bridge. When these services are running in different CoreOS nodes, then these nodes should use the port-mapping functionality provided by the host CoreOS to reach the desired container. But when using this mechanism, the containers should advertise the host machine's IP address in the discovery service. One option to push the host IP to the discovery service is by using the `ExecStartPost` option in the fleet unit file. This way, the container will be able to access the host IP. The host machine IP address and network is not available to the containers. This allows some other external entity to provide this service.

Before looking into how this issue is being solved by mechanisms like Flannel and Weave, let us have a look at the details of Docker container networking.

Introduction to Docker networking

There are multiple communication requirements for containers/service as follows. CoreOS and Docker together should provide a mechanism to meet all the following requirements:

- Container–Container communication in the same CoreOS node
- Container to CoreOS host communication
- Container to external world communication
- Container–Container communication in a different CoreOS node

Let us look into how CoreOS provides these functionalities for the docker container in the following sections.

Container–Container communication

This section describes in detail the different mechanisms provided by the CoreOS and Docker/Container technology to provide communication across different instances of Docker. There are multiple ways to provide this communication as follows:

- Docker0 bridge and veth pair
- Using Link
- Using common network stack

Docker0 bridge and veth pair

Docker0 bridge is a Linux bridge created by docker in order to provide communication across different docker containers. By default, docker creates a Linux bridge called docker0 bridge, which provides connectivity for all the docker containers in the CoreOS host.

 Docker0 bridge is created only at the instantiation of the first container instance. No new bridge will be created on subsequent container instantiation.

Veth is a **Virtual Ethernet Device** that can be used as a virtual link inside the Linux kernel. Typically, the veth device will be created in a pair (called veth pair) to provide connectivity across different instances of a container. When a new container/service is instantiated in the CoreOS node, a new veth pair will be created. One end of the veth pair is attached to the container service and the other end is connected to docker0 bridge. These docker0 bridge and veth pairs provide connectivity across different containers running in the same CoreOS node.

In the following diagram, the docker1 and docker2 containers are connected to docker0 bridge via the veth pair, which provides connectivity across the docker containers. One end of the veth pair, which is attached to the docker instance, will be visible inside the docker instance as the eth0 interface. It is possible to configure the IP address for this eth0 interface. The user can configure the eth0 interface of the docker1 and docker2 instances with the same network in order to provide connectivity across them.

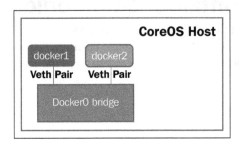

Container–Container communication using docker0 bridge

The docker instances are attached to docker0 bridge using a virtual subnet with an IP address ranging from `172.17.51.1` – `172.17.51.25`. As the docker side of the veth pair gets the IP in the same range, there is a possibility that, in two different servers/VM instances, two containers have the same IP address. This may result in problems while routing the IP packet.

Using Link

This is one of the simple ways of providing communication between Docker containers. **Docker Link** is a unidirectional conduit/pipe between the source and the destination containers. The `docker` command provides a way to link the containers while instantiating the container itself. The `-link` option is used for this purpose. Docker Link can be used only to provide communication between containers running on the same host.

As an example, if the `docker2` container wants to use the networking stack of another container, `docker1`, then the command to start `docker2` is as follows:

```
/usr/bin/docker run --name docker2 –link docker1:docker1 ubuntu /bin/sh
-c "while true; do echo Hello World; sleep 1; done"
```

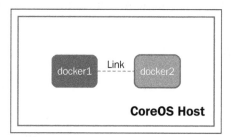

Container–Container communication using Docker Link

Using common network stack

In this mechanism, one docker container will use the networking stack provided by some other docker container's networking stack, instead of having its own networking stack. The docker container will not use the network namespace construct explained in the introduction section of this book, but shares the network namespace with another docker. As the container shares the namespace with another container, any application in one container can communicate with the other container as if both the docker container services are running as an application in one networking stack.

The `docker` command provides a way to use another docker's networking stack while instantiating the container itself. The `-net=container1` option is used for this purpose.

As an example, if the container `cont_net1` wants to use the networking stack of another container, `b1`, then the command to start `cont_net1` is as follows:

```
/usr/bin/docker run -d --name cont_net1 --net= cont_net1:b1 ubuntu /bin/
sh -c "while true; do echo Hello World; sleep 1; done"
```

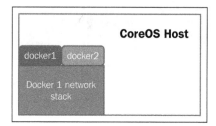

Container–Container communication using common network stack

Container to CoreOS host communication

Apart from the container to container communication mechanism, there are some instances where the service running inside the container may want to talk or exchange some information with applications running in the CoreOS host. CoreOS and docker provide some mechanisms to achieve this using the following mechanisms:

- Host networking
- docker0 bridge

Host networking

In this mechanism, the docker container will use the networking stack provided by the CoreOS host machine instead of having its own networking stack. The docker container will not use the network namespace construct explained in the introduction section of this book, but shares the network namespace with the host CoreOS operating system. As the container shares the namespace with the host CoreOS operating system, any application in the CoreOS host can communicate with the docker container as if the docker container service is running as an application in the CoreOS host. This is one of the simpler mechanisms to allow docker to host communication.

The `docker` command provides a way to use the host machine's networking stack while instantiating the container itself. The `-net=host` option is used for this purpose.

As an example, if the docker1 container wants to use the networking stack of the host CoreOS, then the command to start `docker1` is as follows:

```
/usr/bin/docker run -d --name docker1 --net=host ubuntu_ftp vsftpd
```

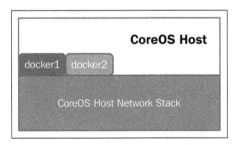

Container–Container communication using the host network stack

docker0 bridge

docker0 bridge can also be used to provide communication between docker and the host operating system. To do this, one of the interfaces in the host operating system should be attached to docker0 bridge, which provides communication. This is illustrated in detail in the following diagram where the `eth1` interface of the CoreOS host machine is also connected to docker0 bridge, which provides connectivity to and from docker and the WAN. In this case, the eth0 interface of docker1, docker2, and the eth1 interface should be in the same network to provide network connectivity between docker and the host CoreOS.

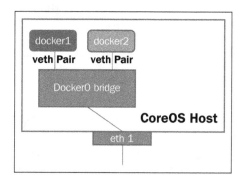

Container – External world communication using docker0 bridge

Container to CoreOS outside world communication

This is one of the basic requirements while deploying a service as a micro-service in the CoreOS cluster. The services running in the CoreOS cluster (as docker) should be accessible from the external world and vice versa. CoreOS and docker provide the following mechanisms to achieve this:

- Host networking
- Port mapping
- Using docker0 bridge

Host networking

Host networking is described in detail in the previous section. As the container shares the namespace with the host CoreOS operating system, when the host CoreOS operating system is connected to WAN, the service running inside the container should also be able to be part of the WAN network.

The `docker` command provides a way to use the host machine's networking stack while instantiating the container itself. The `-net=host` option is used for this purpose.

As an example, if the docker1 container wants to use the networking stack of the host CoreOS, then the command to start docker1 is as follows:

```
/usr/bin/docker run -d --name docker1 --net=host ubuntu_ftp vsftpd
```

Port mapping

This is one of the most widely used mechanisms for communicating a docker container to the external world. In this mechanism, a port number in the host machine will be mapped to a port number in the docker container. Here, the port refers to transport layer ports like UDP port/TCP port. For example, if the user deploys a web server in a docker container, they can map the `HTTP` port (port no. `80`) in the host CoreOS operating system to the `HTTP` port (port no. `80`) of the docker container. So when a HTTP request is received by the CoreOS host, it forwards the request to the container, which processes this HTTP request. But one major challenge with respect to this mechanism is that the same service won't be able to deploy in multiple docker containers, as it results in port collision in the host operating system.

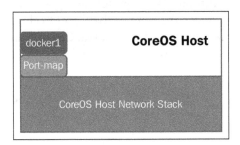

Container – External world communication using port mapping

Container – Container communication in different CoreOS nodes

We have seen how CoreOS or docker provides networking from a single node perspective. As the services are deployed inside the CoreOS cluster, it is necessary to provide communication between containers running in different CoreOS nodes in a cluster. The rest of the chapter discusses this communication mechanism in detail. There are multiple tools that provide this as follows:

- Weave
- Flannel/Rudder
- Using **OVS (OpenVSwitch)**

In this chapter, we are going to see how Flannel and Weave provide the communication mechanism. In the next chapter, we will discuss OVS in detail and how it can be used to provide communication between the various containers.

Introduction to Weave

We learned before that applications running inside Docker have no knowledge of the IP address of the host machine. Hence, they are not in position to register their IP for the service, since another container running outside the host has to use the host IP address for accessing the service.

If an IP address of the host machine is passed as an environment variable, service information can be stored in `etcd` and read by the service user as illustrated in *Chapter 5, Discovering Services Running in Cluster*. This approach requires the application code to be aware of how services can be discovered.

Weave simplifies service discovery and does a lot more. Weave provides a mechanism to connect applications running inside a Docker container irrespective of where they are deployed. Since application services are running as a Docker container, the ease of communication of micro-services running in Docker containers is very important.

Weave registers the named containers automatically in **weaveDNS**, hence services or dockers can be accessed by resolving their names through regular name resolution. This requires application-specific code as routine system calls like `gethostbyname`, or `getaddrinfo` with a pre-defined Docker name used for service, will resolve the name to the IP address using `weaveDNS`.

Weave sets up a Virtual Ethernet Switch connecting all docker containers and in turn services or applications running inside Docker. Weave builds up the network assigning unique IP addresses to each of the docker containers as they come up and free the IP address when they go down. With this, it is no longer required to export a port explicitly when starting Docker and enables service to be accessed from anywhere, thus not making it mandatory that frontend applications run on the host machine, which exposes the public network. It is also possible to assign the IP addresses to the containers manually, which can eventually be used to create isolated subnets. This enables the isolation of a group of applications from another group.

Weave is simple to integrate with Docker, which we will see when we go hands-on later in this chapter. Weave also offers security by encrypting traffic when docker containers need to be connected through public or untrusted networks.

Introduction to Flannel/Rudder

Similar to Weave, **Flannel** also assigns an IP address to a container that can be used for container to container communication by creating an overlay mesh network. Flannel internally uses `etcd` to store the mapping between the assigned container IP address and host IP address. It doesn't have elaborate features like Weave and can be used if other feature sets provided by Weave are not required. For example, Flannel doesn't provide automatic service discovery through DNS and still requires application coding or instrumentation to discover service endpoints.

By default, each container is assigned an IP address in the `/24` subnet. Subnet size can be configured. Flannel uses UDP to encapsulate traffic to transmit to a destination.

In later sections, we will learn about using Flannel. Flannel was previously referred to as **Rudder**.

Integrating Weave with `CoreOSWeave` is rather simple to install. The standalone installation is as simple as pulling the Weave script from the repository and calling another command to set up and start the Weave router.

Let's run through the sequence of command manually, and then we will run the installation and setup through `cloud config`.

Installation

Weave can be installed onto the system by fetching the script using `wget` or `curl`. After downloading, change the permission to make it executable.

```
/usr/bin/wget -N -P /opt/bin git.io/weave
/usr/bin/chmod +x /opt/bin/weave
```

Setting up Weave

Run the command `weave launch` to set up and start the Weave router, Weave DNS, and proxy for Docker API commands like `docker run` and so on. This command also sets up the Weave network. When this command is run for the first time in the machine, the `Weave Docker` image required for setup is downloaded.

```
weave launch
Unable to find image 'weaveworks/weave:latest' locally
latest: Pulling from weaveworks/weave
4c25b19b8af6: Pulling fs layer
6498a5f7a259: Pulling fs layer
638a117dec98: Pulling fs layer
afebf09d0da1: Pulling fs layer
e5ac6ff68d75: Pulling fs layer
6498a5f7a259: Verifying Checksum
6498a5f7a259: Download complete
4c25b19b8af6: Verifying Checksum
4c25b19b8af6: Download complete
638a117dec98: Verifying Checksum
638a117dec98: Download complete
4c25b19b8af6: Pull complete
e5ac6ff68d75: Verifying Checksum
e5ac6ff68d75: Download complete
6498a5f7a259: Pull complete
638a117dec98: Pull complete
afebf09d0da1: Verifying Checksum
afebf09d0da1: Download complete
```

```
afebf09d0da1: Pull complete
e5ac6ff68d75: Pull complete
Digest: sha256:1a8565d24ef2b617619a482cbfe895f8fc27e7a4518ac18b9005ed7b4c
aa223f
Status: Downloaded newer image for weaveworks/weave:latest
```

To check the status, the `status` command is used to check the router status. If this command is run for the first time, the Weave Docker image required for setup is downloaded.

```
weave status
Unable to find image 'weaveworks/weaveexec:latest' locally
latest: Pulling from weaveworks/weaveexec
b6069e3f1ecc: Pull complete
326c397fb7ed: Pull complete
4d2b936d2fa5: Pull complete
16a356f92997: Pull complete
ae09ffb2bf28: Pull complete
14931fda689e: Pull complete
85d81711422f: Pull complete
16bfdc48cfb1: Pull complete
52bab2cc143b: Pull complete
82d8a8c031ec: Pull complete
6993b16a50ae: Pull complete
ee37b21b766d: Pull complete
3c16e5ee0357: Pull complete
77b8fe327374: Pull complete
23272d8d46c3: Pull complete
Digest: sha256:1d34246eb53f070f0e35ad13974367e2a4fee78039da74b8760a4eff49
a9334f
Status: Downloaded newer image for weaveworks/weaveexec:latest
        Version: git-efd4fc4704ce

    Service: router
   Protocol: weave 1..2
       Name: 5a:62:3a:91:af:c5(core-01.testdomain.com)
```

```
     Encryption: disabled
  PeerDiscovery: enabled
        Targets: 0
    Connections: 0
          Peers: 1
 TrustedSubnets: none

        Service: ipam
         Status: idle
          Range: 10.32.0.0-10.47.255.255
  DefaultSubnet: 10.32.0.0/12

        Service: dns
         Domain: weave.local.
       Upstream: 10.0.2.3
            TTL: 1
        Entries: 0

        Service: proxy
        Address: unix:///var/run/weave/weave.sock
```

If specific IP addresses were not provided during container startup, Weave assigns a free IP from the address pool to the container and releases that address (that is, marks it free) when the container exits. The IP address pool is maintained across all the Weave instances that are part of the cluster. Hence, at Weave launch either all the members of the cluster or one or more members of the cluster should be provided. Additionally, a parameter should be included to inform Weave about the number of members. To illustrate, if there are three members with the IP addresses `172.17.8.101`, `172.17.8.102`, and `172.17.8.103` then the following commands are the right way to launch Weave for allocating the IP addresses.

Option one:

```
core@core-01 ~$ weave launch 172.17.8.102 172.17.8.103
core@core-02 ~$ weave launch 172.17.8.101 172.17.8.103
core@core-03 ~$ weave launch 172.17.8.101 172.17.8.102
```

Option two:

```
core@core-01 ~$ weave launch --init-peer-count 3
core@core-02 ~$ weave launch --init-peer-count 3 172.17.8.101
core@core-03 ~$ weave launch --init-peer-count 3 172.17.8.102
```

Weave allocates IP addresses in the `10.32.0.0/12` range by default, unless it's overridden with the `--ipalloc-range` option at the time of launch. For instance, if the subnet to be used is `10.1.0.0` with a size of `16`, the following command can be provided. The same value should be provided across all the members.

```
weave launch --ipalloc-range 10.1.0.0/16
```

Weave gives an option to enable or disable the use of the Weave DNS service. By default, the Weave DNS service is enabled. To disable this service, the `--without-dns` option can be provided while running Weave. Weave maintains an in-memory database of all the hosts. It builds up the database as the peer join. This is maintained on all the hosts and is replicated across hosts. If a hostname is in the `.weave.local` domain, then Weave DNS records the association of that name with the container's Weave IP address (es). When DNS query arrives for the `.weave.local` domain, the Weave DNS database is used to return with the IPs of all containers for that hostname across the entire cluster. When DNS query arrives for the name in a domain other than `.weave.local`, it queries the host's configured nameserver, hence complying with default behavior.

Container startup

Docker containers can be started by using the Weave proxy or without using the Weave proxy. When containers are created using the Weave proxy, the container initialization waits for the Weave network interface to become available and then proceeds with further startup of the container. The IP addresses of the containers are assigned and the container is connected to the Weave network.

The following command sets up the environment so that Docker containers can connect to the Weave network automatically. The usual Docker commands can be used to start the Docker container:

```
eval "$(weave env)"
docker run ...
```

By default, Weave allows the communication of a container with all other containers in the cluster. This can be restricted by providing a subnet range from which an IP address can be allocated. Multiple subnets can also be provided. Also, an IP address can be provided that will be assigned to the container in addition to the automatic IP address allocation. It is also possible to avoid automatic IP address allocation:

```
docker run -e WEAVE_CIDR=net:10.32.7.0/24 ...
docker run -e WEAVE_CIDR="net:10.32.1.0/24 net:10.32.8.0/24
ip:10.32.9.1/24" ...
```

Containers can be launched without the Weave proxy by starting them using the command `weave run`.

The following is the setup that will be used to illustrate a network between two CoreOS hosts. We will instantiate two CoreOS members in a cluster and spawn two docker containers inside members. The docker container runs a busybox shell so that we can run the networking command and check the IP address assignments and peer container reachability. This setup illustrates the scenario where communication is happening between docker containers across two CoreOS hosts.

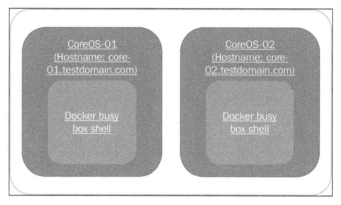

Weave setup

The following is the `cloud-config` file used to create the setup. The other configuration files reused are from the section *Static discovery* in *Chapter 3, Creating your CoreOS cluster and managing the Cluster*. Set `$num_instances` to 2 in the `config.rb` file as we need to start only two instances of members.

```
#cloud-config

---
write_files:
```

```
      - path: /etc/weave.core-01.testdomain.com.env
        permissions: 0644
        owner: root
        content: |
          WEAVE_LAUNCH_ARGS="172.17.8.102"
      - path: /etc/weave.core-02.testdomain.com.env
        permissions: 0644
        owner: root
        content: |
          WEAVE_LAUNCH_ARGS="172.17.8.101"

  coreos:
    units:
      - name: 10-weave.network
        runtime: false
        content: |
          [Match]
          Type=bridge
          Name=weave*

          [Network]

      - name: install-weave.service
        command: start
        enable: true
        content: |
          [Unit]
          After=network-online.target
          After=docker.service
          Description=Install Weave
          Requires=network-online.target
          Requires=docker.service

          [Service]
          Type=oneshot
          RemainAfterExit=yes
          ExecStartPre=/usr/bin/wget -N -P /opt/bin git.io/weave
          ExecStartPre=/usr/bin/chmod +x /opt/bin/weave
          ExecStart=/bin/echo Wave Installed

      - name: weave.service
        command: start
```

```
    enable: true
    content: |
      [Unit]
      After=install-weave.service
      Description=Weave Network
      Requires=install-weave.service

      [Service]
      Type=oneshot
      EnvironmentFile=/etc/weave.%H.env
      ExecStart=/opt/bin/weave launch $WEAVE_LAUNCH_ARGS
```

Let's run through the finer details of the `cloud-config` file before we start containers in the members and check connectivity.

Firstly, we create two files using the `write_files` section. They will be used before starting Weave on respective machines. Each file has the hostname in their name, so that using `%H` in `EnvironmentFile` results in referring the file meant for the member.

Unit file `10-weave.network` is added to allow the Weave network to be used for DHCP queries. By default, `docker0` bridge is used. This is optional and is required if the Weave network is being used for DHCP.

Unit `install-weave.service` installs Weave onto the member and sets the required permissions. This is a one-shot service as it has served its purpose once Weave is installed. `After=network-online.target` is added to ensure that this network is up before Weave is installed. This is required so that packages can be downloaded from the Internet.

Unit `weave.service` sources the corresponding environment file and launches Weave.

Boot the cluster using `Vagrant up`. After booting up, the nodes in the cluster comes up with weave networking up:

```
vagrant ssh core-01
weave status

        Version: 1.4.2

        Service: router
```

```
       Protocol: weave 1..2
           Name: 96:63:f1:5a:ac:3a(core-01.testdomain.com)
     Encryption: disabled
  PeerDiscovery: enabled
        Targets: 0
    Connections: 1 (1 established)
          Peers: 2 (with 2 established connections)
 TrustedSubnets: none

        Service: ipam
         Status: idle
          Range: 10.32.0.0-10.47.255.255
  DefaultSubnet: 10.32.0.0/12

        Service: dns
         Domain: weave.local.
       Upstream: 10.0.2.3
            TTL: 1
        Entries: 0

        Service: proxy
        Address: unix:///var/run/weave/weave.sock
```

We can see that both the peers are connected. We can also see that the DNS and router services are enabled with default settings.

Now we will start a Docker container on each of the members. We will run a simple shell on busybox. The following command is executed on both the members. Note that we are providing the name of the docker container explicitly. This will result in two DNS entries with the domain .weave.local.

```
vagrant ssh core-01
eval "$(weave env)"
/usr/bin/docker run --name=container2 -it busybox /bin/sh
/ # ifconfig -a
...
```

```
ethwe      Link encap:Ethernet  HWaddr E6:AA:25:26:EA:04
           inet addr:10.32.0.1  Bcast:0.0.0.0  Mask:255.240.0.0
           inet6 addr: fe80::e4aa:25ff:fe26:ea04/64 Scope:Link
           UP BROADCAST RUNNING MULTICAST  MTU:1410  Metric:1
           RX packets:13 errors:0 dropped:0 overruns:0 frame:0
           TX packets:8 errors:0 dropped:0 overruns:0 carrier:0
           collisions:0 txqueuelen:1000
           RX bytes:1385 (1.3 KiB)  TX bytes:620 (620.0 B)
...


vagrant ssh core-02
eval "$(weave env)"
/usr/bin/docker run --name=container2 -it busybox /bin/sh
/ # ifconfig -a
...

ethwe      Link encap:Ethernet  HWaddr DA:E1:B8:3A:39:FB
           inet addr:10.40.0.0  Bcast:0.0.0.0  Mask:255.240.0.0
           inet6 addr: fe80::d8e1:b8ff:fe3a:39fb/64 Scope:Link
           UP BROADCAST RUNNING MULTICAST  MTU:1410  Metric:1
           RX packets:11 errors:0 dropped:0 overruns:0 frame:0
           TX packets:7 errors:0 dropped:0 overruns:0 carrier:0
           collisions:0 txqueuelen:1000
           RX bytes:969 (969.0 B)  TX bytes:550 (550.0 B)
...
```

Now ping the IP address and hostname of the other container to ensure that the network across containers and the DNS service is working. You can also run the status command to check that two DNS entries has been updated, once the containers are started.

```
weave status
...
        Service: dns
         Domain: weave.local.
       Upstream: 10.0.2.3
```

```
      TTL: 1

  Entries: 2


  Service: proxy
  Address: unix:///var/run/weave/weave.sock
```

Integrating Flannel with CoreOS

Flannel runs a daemon `flanneld` on each host, responsible for allocating a free IP within the configured subnet. `flanneld` sets a watch on `etcd` information and routes the packets using the mechanism configured.

Although the `flanneld` service is not part of the standard CoreOS distribution, when the `flanneld` service is started through `cloud-config`, CoreOS internally starts a service before other initializations to pull `flanneld` from the `docker` registry. `flanneld` is stored as a `docker` container in the CoreOS enterprise registry.

The same setup used for Weave networking is being used here. Note that for Flannel, hostnames are irrelevant.

The following is the `cloud-config` file used to create setup. The other configuration files are reused from the *Static discovery* section in *Chapter 3, Creating your CoreOS cluster and Managing the Cluster.* Set $num_instances to 2 in the `config.rb` file as we need to start only two instance of members.

```
#cloud-config

---
coreos:
  etcd2:
    name: core-03
    advertise-client-urls: http://$public_ipv4:2379
    initial-advertise-peer-urls: http://$private_ipv4:2380
    listen-client-urls: http://0.0.0.0:2379,http://0.0.0.0:4001
    listen-peer-urls: http://$private_ipv4:2380,http://$private_
ipv4:7001
    initial-cluster-token: coreOS-static
    initial-cluster: core-01=http://172.17.8.101:2380,core-
02=http://172.17.8.102:2380,core-03=http://172.17.8.103:2380
  flannel:
    interface: $public_ipv4
```

```
units:
  - name: etcd2.service
    command: start
    enable: true
  - name: flanneld.service
    drop-ins:
      - name: 50-network-config.conf
        content: |
          [Service]
          ExecStartPre=/usr/bin/etcdctl set /coreos.com/network/config
'{ "Network": "10.1.0.0/16" }'
    command: start
```

Vagrant setup will configure the interface that Flannel should use. This is done by providing the following configuration in `cloud-config`:

```
flannel:
    interface: $public_ipv4
```

Directive ExecStartPre is added to the flanneld service configuration as a drop-in file with the name 50-network-config.conf. Using ExecStartPre, Flannel configuration is updated in etcd. This is mandatory for Flannel to work as it looks up the configuration at /coreos.com/network/config. The following are the Flannel configurations that can be provided as comma-separated values while setting the configuration to etcd:

- Network: This specifies the subnets to be used across all Flannel networks. This field is mandatory. In the preceding example, the subnet configuration was provided as 10.1.0.0/16. Further subnets for each of the hosts will be created within this subnet.

- SubnetLen: This specifies the size of the subnet as bits allocated to each host. This field should have a value less or equal to the subnet size provided for the network. If this field is not provided, a default value of 24 is used if the Network field has a subnet size more than or equal to 24. If the Network field has a subnet size less than 24 and this field is not configured, one less than the value configured for the Network is used.

- SubnetMin: This specifies the starting IP range from which the subnet allocation starts. This defaults to the first subnet of Network if this field is not provided.

- SubnetMax: This specifies the end IP range from which the subnet allocation starts. This defaults to the first subnet of Network if this field is not provided.

- Backend: This specifies the mechanism to be used for sending traffic across hosts. Supported values are udp, vxlan, host-gw, and so on. If this field is not provided, udp is used. If udp is used, the port number to be used for UDP is configured. If the port is not provided, the default port of 8285 is used. This port should be allowed if the hosts are to be networked across firewalls.

The following is another sample configuration for Flannel, which contains other optional parameters set to their respective defaults:

```
ExecStartPre=/usr/bin/etcdctl set /coreos.com/network/config '{
"Network": "10.1.0.0/16", "SubnetLen": 24, "SubnetMin": "10.1.0.0",
"SubnetMax": "10.1.255.0"}'
```

Boot the cluster using Vagrant up. After booting up, the clusters come up with the interfaces setup on the host by Flannel.

```
vagrant ssh core-01

ifconfig -a

...

flannel0: flags=4305<UP,POINTOPOINT,RUNNING,NOARP,MULTICAST>  mtu 1472
        inet 10.1.35.0  netmask 255.255.0.0  destination 10.1.35.0
        unspec 00-00-00-00-00-00-00-00-00-00-00-00-00-00-00-00
txqueuelen 500  (UNSPEC)
        RX packets 0  bytes 0 (0.0 B)
        RX errors 0  dropped 0  overruns 0  frame 0
        TX packets 0  bytes 0 (0.0 B)
        TX errors 0  dropped 0 overruns 0  carrier 0  collisions 0


...
```

Similarly, we can see that interfaces were created by Flannel on other instances also.

```
vagrant ssh core-02

ifconfig -a

...

flannel0: flags=4305<UP,POINTOPOINT,RUNNING,NOARP,MULTICAST>  mtu 1472
```

```
        inet 10.1.27.0  netmask 255.255.0.0  destination 10.1.27.0

        unspec 00-00-00-00-00-00-00-00-00-00-00-00-00-00-00-00
txqueuelen 500  (UNSPEC)

        RX packets 0  bytes 0 (0.0 B)

        RX errors 0  dropped 0  overruns 0  frame 0

        TX packets 0  bytes 0 (0.0 B)

        TX errors 0  dropped 0 overruns 0  carrier 0  collisions 0
```

...

Flannel sets up subnets `10.1.35.0` for host1 and `10.1.27.0` for host2 to be used by containers. Flannel decides on the available subnets before allocating to a host. Now, we will start a `Docker` container on each of the members. We will run a simple shell on `busybox`. The following command is executed on both the members:

```
vagrant ssh core-01
/usr/bin/docker run -it busybox /bin/sh
/ # ifconfig -a
eth0      Link encap:Ethernet  HWaddr 02:42:0A:01:23:03
          inet addr:10.1.35.3  Bcast:0.0.0.0  Mask:255.255.255.0
          inet6 addr: fe80::42:aff:fe01:2303/64 Scope:Link
          UP BROADCAST RUNNING MULTICAST  MTU:1472  Metric:1
          RX packets:19 errors:0 dropped:0 overruns:0 frame:0
          TX packets:6 errors:0 dropped:0 overruns:0 carrier:0
          collisions:0 txqueuelen:0
          RX bytes:1611 (1.5 KiB)  TX bytes:508 (508.0 B)
```

...

```
vagrant ssh core-02
/usr/bin/docker run -it busybox /bin/sh
/ # ifconfig -a
eth0      Link encap:Ethernet  HWaddr 02:42:0A:01:1B:03
          inet addr:10.1.27.3  Bcast:0.0.0.0  Mask:255.255.255.0
          inet6 addr: fe80::42:aff:fe01:1b03/64 Scope:Link
          UP BROADCAST RUNNING MULTICAST  MTU:1472  Metric:1
          RX packets:21 errors:0 dropped:0 overruns:0 frame:0
```

```
TX packets:9 errors:0 dropped:0 overruns:0 carrier:0
collisions:0 txqueuelen:0
RX bytes:1751 (1.7 KiB)   TX bytes:738 (738.0 B)
```

. . .

As we see, an IP address from the corresponding subnet of the hosts has been allocated to the container and the IP addresses can be pinged from the other container. This also illustrates that with add-ons like Weave and Flannel, communication across containers is much simpler and closer to the communication of applications across bare metal.

Summary

In this chapter, we have seen the importance of container communications and the various possibilities provided by CoreOS and docker to provide the communication. In the next chapter, we are going to see how **OVS (OpenVSwitch)** can be used to provide the communication mechanism over an underlay network. Apart from Flannel, Weave, and OVS, there are other mechanisms like pipework available to provision the network inside the CoreOS and docker environment.

7
Creating a Virtual Tenant Network and Service Chaining Using OVS

In the previous chapter, we saw how different services running inside the CoreOS cluster can be linked with each other. The chapter described in detail how the services deployed by different customers/tenants across the CoreOS cluster can be linked/connected using OVS.

This chapter covers the following topics:

- Introduction to OpenVSwitch/OVS
- Introduction to overlay and underlay networks
- Introduction to virtual tenant networks
- Docker networking using OVS

As OVS is a production-quality, widely deployed software switch with a wide range of feature sets, we are going to see how OVS can be used to provide service chaining, which can differentiate between different customer services.

Introduction to OVS

OpenVSwitch (OVS) is a production-quality open source virtual switch application that can be run on any Unix-based systems. Typically, OVS is used in a virtualization environment to provide communication between the virtual machines/containers that are running inside the servers. OVS acts as a software switch that provides layer2 connectivity between the VMs running inside a server. Linux Bridge can also be used for providing communication between the VMs inside the server. However, OVS provides all the bells and whistles that are required in a typical server virtualization environment. The following diagram depicts how OVS provides connectivity across the VMs running inside the server:

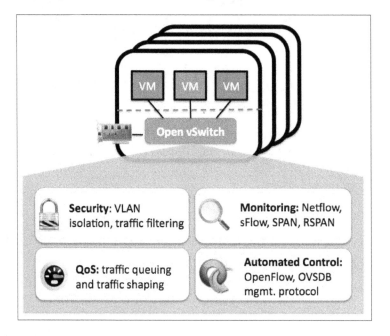

In the diagram, there are three VMs that are running in a server. One end of the VM's virtual NIC is connected to **Open vSwitch**. Here, **Open vSwitch** provides connectivity across all the VMs in the server. **Open vSwitch** is also connected to the physical NIC to provide communication to and from the VMs to the external world.

The OVS offers **Security** by providing traffic **isolation** using **VLAN** and **traffic filtering** based on various packet headers. OVS provides a way for **Monitoring** the packets that are exchanged across the VMs in the server using protocols like **sFlow**, **SPAN, RSPAN**, and so on. OVS also supports **QoS** (quality of service) with **traffic queuing and shaping** along with **OpenFlow** support.

OVS architectural overview

This section describes the high-level architectural overview of OVS and its components.

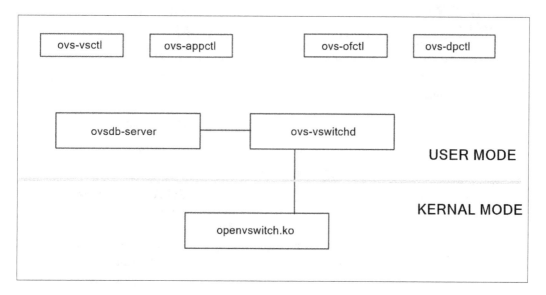

The main components of OVS are as follows:

- `ovs-vsctl`: This is the utility provided by OVS for configuring and querying the `ovs-vswitchd` daemon via `ovsdb-server`

- `ovs-appctl`: This is a utility for managing the logging level of OVS

- `ovs-ofctl`: This is the utility provided by OVS for managing OpenFlow entries in the switch

- `ovs-dpctl`: This is the data-path management utility that is used to configure the data path of OVS

- `ovsdb-server`: This is the DB that stores persistently all the configurations of OVS

- `ovs-vswitchd`: This is the OVS switchd module that provides the core functionality, such as bridging, VLAN segregation, and so on of OVS

- `Openvswitch.ko`: This is the data-path module for handling fast switching and tunneling of traffic

Advantages of using OVS in CoreOS

In a CoreOS environment, OVS can replace docker0 bridge and can provide connectivity across the different containers in the CoreOS instance. docker0 bridge can only provide connectivity across the containers running in the same CoreOS instance. However, along with providing connectivity across the containers running in the same CoreOS instance, OVS can be used to provide connectivity across the containers running in different CoreOS instances. The following are the key advantages provided by OVS compared to other techniques mentioned in the previous chapter:

- As the name implies, OpenVSwitch/OVS does layer2 bridging/switching of data from one container to other containers. It does typical layer2 processing, such as flooding, learning, forwarding, traffic segregation based on VLAN tag, providing loop-free topology using spanning tree protocol, and so on.

- OVS supports tunneling protocols, such as GRE, VxLAN, and so on. These are the tunneling protocols that are used to carry layer2 traffic over a layer3 network. These tunnels are used to provide connectivity for containers running in different CoreOS instances. The VxLAN protocol is defined in detail in RFC 7348 and the GRE protocol is defined in detail in RFC 2784. These tunnels provide the virtual infrastructure for laying out the overlay network over the physical underlay network.

- OVS also supports the OpenFlow protocol that can be programmed by an external SDN controller like OpenDayLight Controller, RYU Controller, ONOS controller, and so on. This means the CoreOS cluster can be managed easily by a centralized controller in a typical SDN deployment.

Before looking in detail at how OVS can be used to provide connectivity across containers and hence can provide service chaining, we may need to look into some of the core concepts and features, such as overlay network, underlay network, and Virtual Tenant Network.

Introduction to overlay and underlay networks

The following diagram represents the typical service provided by OVS in a virtual machine environment:

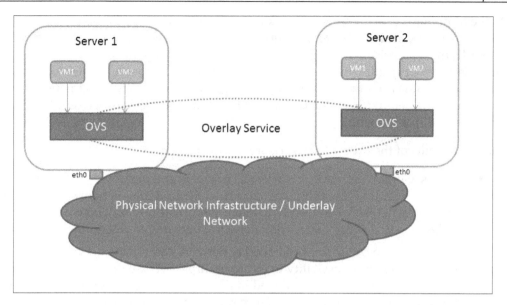

Server1 and Server2 are the two physical servers wherein the customer applications are deployed inside the VM. There are two VMs in each server as VM1 and VM2. The green VM belongs to one customer and the orange VM belongs to another customer. A single instance of OVS is running in each of the servers.

In a typical virtualization environment, there are two kinds of network devices: the soft switch, which provides connectivity to the virtualization layer, and the physical switch, which provides connectivity to the physical infrastructure (such as servers, switches, and routers).

The OVS switch provides connectivity to the VMs/containers running inside the server instance. These server instances are also connected to each other physically in order to provide connectivity for all the servers.

The physical network that provides connectivity for the servers is termed the underlay network. This underlay network will have the physical infrastructure that comprises physical switches and routers, which provides connectivity for the servers.

Now, the complexity comes in providing connectivity across the containers that are running in the server to other containers that are running in different server instances. There are multiple solutions to solve this problem. One of the major and widely deployed solutions is using OVS to provide the overlay network.

As the term implies, an overlay network is a network that is overlaid on top of another network. Unlike physical underlay networks, overlay networks are virtual networks that comprise virtual links that share an underlying physical network (underlay network), allowing deployment of containers/virtual machines to provide connectivity with each other without the need to modify the underlying network. The virtual link here refers to the tunnels that provide connectivity across OVS. OVS supports multiple tunneling protocols; widely used tunnels are GRE and VxLAN.

The key benefits of the overlay network are:

- As it is a logical network, it is possible to create and destroy the overlay network very easily without any change in the underlay networks. To create an overlay network between two nodes, just create a tunnel between the nodes, and to destroy the overlay network, unconfigure the tunnel interface.

- It is possible to create multiple overlay networks across the nodes. For instance, there is a possibility to create multiple overlay networks based on the number of customers deployed in a server instance. This provides a way of virtualizing the network similar to server virtualization. Let us look into the details of network virtualization.

Introduction to network virtualization

Network virtualization is one of the most widely discussed topics in the recent past in the networking industry. To understand network virtualization better, think of server virtualization wherein the physical infrastructures are logically segregated into multiple virtual devices, each assigning to different containers for performing its workload. Similar to server virtualization, there is a requirement to virtualize the networking layer that provides connectivity for different virtual machines/containers.

As in server virtualization, wherein the customer will have full access to the virtualized server infrastructure, customers may also want to virtualize the networking infrastructure to secure data traffic between their VMs or containers. They don't want others to expose the data exchange that is happening between their applications to other customers' VMs or containers.

Network virtualization as a concept is not new to the networking world. Network virtualization is realized in existing networks using technologies or concepts such as VLAN, VRF, L2VPN, L3VPN, and so on. These network virtualization techniques provide a mechanism for isolating traffic from one customer to another customer. VLAN provides a way of logically segregating the layer2 broadcast domain based on the VLAN tag.

These technologies also define the necessary protocol support to have overlapping address spaces across different customers. Say, for instance, using VRF, it is possible for two or more customers to use and share their IP address across different sites.

However, these technologies are not providing true network virtualization throughout the network. These technologies also have their own limitations. The 1026 number of VLAN limits the number of tenants in the network. Similarly for VPN support, protocols like MPLS may be required that are typically deployed in a service provider network.

As more and more operators and cloud providers are deploying **Software Defined Networking (SDN)** and **Network Function Virtualization (NFV)**, it is necessary to provide a mechanism to provide network virtualization and traffic isolation in a better way.

The overlay network described in the previous chapter can provide an effective mechanism to isolate data traffic across different tenants or customers. As multiple overlay networks (one for each different customer) can be laid out over the underlay physical infrastructure, we should be able to provide the required traffic isolation between different customer traffic. Hence, the overlay network infrastructure provides an easy way of providing network virtualization.

To create an overlay network for a customer or tenant, we need to create a tunnel across all the nodes wherein the customer's/tenant's application is deployed. OVS helps in creating a tunnel across the different OVS instances and hence supports the creation of VTNs and underlay networks.

Going back to the previous diagram, there are two customers, shown as green and orange. Both customers' VMs are running in both server1 and server2. In order to provide network virtualization and isolate the traffic across these two customers, the following steps can be used:

- Create two bridge instances in OVS, one for each customer, as Greenbr and Orangebr.

- Attach the VM's virtual NIC interface (veth) to the corresponding bridge instance. For example, the green VM's virtual NIC should be attached to Greenbr and the orange VM's virtual NIC interface should be attached to Orangebr.

- Create two tunnels, say `Green_tun` and `Orange_tun`, between server1 and server2. The two server instances can be part of the same network or different networks. If they are part of different networks, one or more routers should be deployed to provide physical connectivity between these servers.

To create a tunnel between two nodes, there should be IP reachability between these two nodes. IP reachability will be provided by the underlay network.

• Attach these two tunnels to the respective bridge instances.

With these simple steps, it is possible to create a virtual network for different customers. This is illustrated in the following diagram:

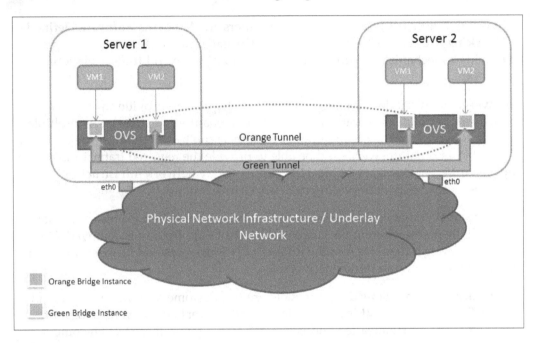

OpenFlow support in OVS

One of the key advantages of using OVS is that it supports the OpenFlow protocol and supports flow-based switching. **OpenFlow** is a protocol defined by ONF to manage the network infrastructure centrally with standard interfaces between the controller (traditionally called the control plane) and the actual packet-forwarding entity (traditionally called the data plane). Enabling the network to be programmed centrally makes the whole system more agile and flexible.

OpenFlow promises to ease the way of provisioning large data centers and server clusters that can be managed centrally using OpenFlow controllers. With large data centers and server clusters, there is a clear necessity of changing the traditional control plane and data plane paradigm to move toward flow-based switching, which is more generic and can be adoptable for different avenues. Software Defined Networking (SDN) is a new paradigm shift in networking.

The OpenFlow specification defines three different components in an OpenFlow-based network as follows.

OpenFlow switch

An **OpenFlow switch** consists of one or more flow tables, meter table, group table, and OpenFlow channels to the external controller. The flow tables and group table are used during the lookup or forwarding phase of packet pipeline processing in order to forward the packet to the appropriate port, whereas the meter table is used to perform simple QoS operations, such as rate-limiting to complex QOS operations, such as DiffServ and so on. The switch communicates with the controller and the controller manages the switch via the OpenFlow protocol using OpenFlow messages.

OpenFlow controller

An **OpenFlow controller** typically manages one or more OpenFlow switches remotely via OpenFlow channels. Similarly, a single switch can be managed by multiple controllers for better reliability and better load balancing. The OpenFlow controller acts in a similar way to the control plane of typical traditional switches or routers. The controller is responsible for programming various tables, such as flow table, group table, and meter table using OpenFlow protocol messages to provide network connectivity or network functions across various nodes in the system

OpenFlow channel

An **OpenFlow channel** is used to exchange OpenFlow messages between an OpenFlow switch and an OpenFlow controller. The switch must be able to create an OpenFlow channel by initiating a connection to the controller:

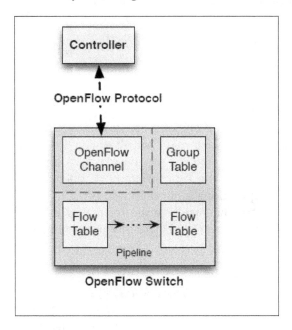

With OVS, the entire CoreOS cluster's overlay network can be centrally managed by a controller with very simple configurations. The ofctl utility provided by OVS is helpful in programming the flow tables using a command-line argument without being controlled by an external controller.

Running OVS in CoreOS

There are two ways to run or install OVS in a CoreOS environment:

- Build a CoreOS image with OVS
- Run OVS inside a Docker container with the -net=host option

As we have already seen in *Chapter 1, CoreOS, Yet Another Linux Distro* in CoreOS there is no way to install an application. Any service/application should be deployed in a container. So the simple way to run OVS is to run OVS inside a Docker container. Let us see how we can install an OVS docker in CoreOS.

There is already a docker image available with OVS (coreos-ovs). Download this docker image from `https://github.com/theojulienne/coreos-ovs` github link. Use the following `cloud-config` to start this container:

`#cloud-config`

```
coreos:
  units:
    - name: docker.service
      command: start
      drop-ins:
        - name: 50-custom-bridge.conf
          content: |
            [Service]
            Environment='DOCKER_OPTS=--bip="10.0.11.0/8" --fixed-
            cidr="10.0.11.0/24"'
    - name: OVS.service
      command: start
      content: |
        [Unit]
        Description=Open vSwitch Bridge
        After=docker.service
        Requires=docker.service

        [Service]
        Restart=always
        ExecStartPre=/sbin/modprobe openvswitch
        ExecStartPre=/sbin/modprobe af_key
        ExecStartPre=-/usr/bin/docker run --name=openvswitch-cfg -v
        /opt/ovs/etc busybox true
        ExecStartPre=-/usr/bin/docker rm -f openvswitch
        ExecStartPre=/usr/bin/docker run -d --net=host --privileged -
        -name=openvswitch --volumes-from=openvswitch-cfg
        theojulienne/coreos-ovs:latest
        ExecStart=/usr/bin/docker attach openvswitch
        ExecStartPost=/usr/bin/docker exec openvswitch
        /scripts/docker-attach
```

This starts a docker container that has OVS installed. Along with that, it removes the IP address of docker0 bridge and assigns it to OVS bridge (bridge0). docker0 bridge will be attached to bridge0 as a link.

As we are using the `-net=host` option, any OVS command we are executing inside this container will result in changing the network configuration of the host OS, which is the CoreOS network stack.

This section describes in detail how to provide a virtual tenant network between docker containers that are running in two different CoreOS instances. There are multiple ways to provide the solution. We are going to see the two most common and simple ways of providing the solution:

- Attaching docker0 bridge to OVS
- Attaching the container's veth interface to OVS

Attaching docker0 bridge to OVS

This is a simple way of providing connectivity across different containers using OVS. In this case, OVS should be connected to docker0 bridge (which is already connected to all the containers) using a veth interface. Refer to the previous chapter for more detail about docker0 bridge and how it provides connectivity for the containers in a system.

The docker bridge is intern connected to the OVS bridge. The OVS bridge provides connectivity to the other CoreOS instances using GRE/VxLAN tunnels.

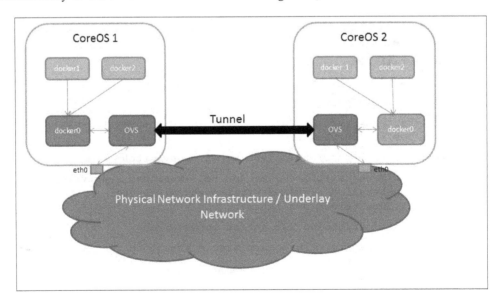

The step-by-step procedure with configuration is described in detail as follows. This consists of the following major steps on both the CoreOS instances:

- Configurations during the instantiation of a CoreOS node in a cluster
- Configurations during the creation of a container

Configuration in CoreOS Instance 1

This section describes in detail the operations to be performed on the coreos-ovs docker of CoreOS node1 to provide this solution.

Configurations during the instantiation of a CoreOS node 1 in a cluster

At the time of CoreOS server boot-up, OVS needs to be started and the procedure to start OVS is as follows. Note that the way in which the OVS command will be executed depends on whether OVS is deployed inside a docker container or the CoreOS host instance. However, in both cases, there is no change in the list of OVS commands to be used:

1. Run the OVS data-path module using the command:

   ```
   sudo modprobe openvswitch
   ```

2. Create a configuration, db, using the default schema file with the following command:

   ```
   sudo ovsdb-tool create /var/lib/openvswitch/conf.db /usr/share/
   openvswitch/vswitch.ovsschema
   ```

3. Run the OVS DB server using the following command:

   ```
   sudo ovsdb-server /var/lib/openvswitch/conf.db --remote=punix:/
   var/run/openvswitch/db.sock --pidfile --detach --log-file
   ```

4. Run OVS-VSCTL using the following command:

   ```
   sudo ovs-vsctl --no-wait init
   ```

5. Run the OVS switchd daemon using the following command:

   ```
   sudo ovs-vswitchd --pidfile --detach
   ```

6. Create a bridge instance:

   ```
   sudo ovs-vsctl add-br br0
   ```

7. Create a GRE tunnel with the remote node as `172.17.8.103`. Here, the assumption is the etho IP of CoreOS instance 2 is `172.17.8.103`:

```
sudo ovs-vsctl add-port br0 gre1 -- set Interface gre1 type=gre
options:remote_ip=172.17.8.103 options:key=100
```

 The key needs to be different for each tunnel.

8. Create a veth interface to provide a connection between docker0 bridge and OVS:

   ◦ Create the veth pair:
   ```
   ip link add tap1 type veth peer name tap2
   ```

   ◦ Attach one end of the veth pair to docker0 bridge:
   ```
   sudo brctl addif docker0 tap1
   ```

   ◦ Attach the other end of the veth pair to OVS:
   ```
   sudo ovs-vsctl add-port br0 tap2
   ```

Configurations during the creation of a container for CoreOS Instance 1

This section describes the configuration to be done when a new container is created in the CoreOS instance.

 As by default, the eth0 (one end of the veth pair) interface of the container is attached to docker0 bridge, we need not explicitly attach the container veth interface to docker0 bridge.

Set the IP address of the eth0 interface of the docker container. It is not possible to set the IP address of the docker container inside the docker instance. We need to use the `nsenter` utility for this. To do this, follow these steps:

1. Execute the following command and get the `pid`:
   ```
   docker inspect --format {{.State.Pid}} <container_name_or_ID>
   ```

2. Execute the following command and get the `pid`:
   ```
   sudo nsenter --target $PID --mount --uts --ipc --net --pid
   ifconfig eth0 50.0.0.1
   ```

Configuration in CoreOS Instance 2

This section describes in detail the operations to be performed on the coreos-ovs docker of CoreOS node2 to provide this solution.

Configurations during the instantiation of CoreOS node 2 in a cluster

This section describes the list of operations to be performed during the initialization of the CoreOS instance. During initialization, OVS needs to be started and the procedure to start OVS is as follows:

- Run the OVS data-path module using the command:

  ```
  sudo modprobe openvswitch
  ```

- Create a configuration, db, using the default schema file with the following command:

  ```
  sudo ovsdb-tool create /var/lib/openvswitch/conf.db /usr/share/
  openvswitch/vswitch.ovsschema
  ```

- Run the OVS DB server using the following command:

  ```
  sudo ovsdb-server /var/lib/openvswitch/conf.db --remote=punix:/
  var/run/openvswitch/db.sock --pidfile --detach --log-file
  ```

- Run OVS-VSCTL using the following command:

  ```
  sudo ovs-vsctl --no-wait init
  ```

- Run the OVS switchd daemon using the following command:

  ```
  sudo ovs-vswitchd --pidfile --detach
  ```

- Create a bridge instance:

  ```
  sudo ovs-vsctl add-br br0
  ```

- Create a GRE tunnel with the remote node as `172.17.8.101`. Here, the assumption is the etho IP of CoreOS instance 1 is `172.17.8.101`:

  ```
  sudo ovs-vsctl add-port br0 gre1 -- set Interface gre1 type=gre
  options:remote_ip=172.17.8.101 options:key=100
  ```

 The key needs to be different for each tunnel.

- Now we need to create a veth interface to provide a connection between docker0 bridge and OVS:

  - Create the veth pair:
    ```
    ip link add tap1 type veth peer name tap2
    ```

  - Attach one end of the veth pair to docker0 bridge:
    ```
    sudo brctl addif docker0 tap1
    ```

  - Attach the other end of the veth pair to OVS:
    ```
    sudo ovs-vsctl add-port br0 tap2
    ```

Configurations during the creation of a container for CoreOS Instance 2

This section describes the configuration to be done when a new container is created in the CoreOS instance.

Set the IP address of the eth0 interface of the docker container. It is not possible to set the IP address of the docker container inside the docker instance. We need to use the `nsenter` utility for this. To do this, follow these steps:

1. Execute the following command and get the pid:
   ```
   docker inspect --format {{.State.Pid}} <container_name_or_ID>
   ```

2. Execute the following command and get the pid:
   ```
   sudo nsenter --target $PID --mount --uts --ipc --net --pid
   ifconfig eth0 50.0.0.2
   ```

Now you should be able to ping from the docker container running in CoreOS instance 1 to a docker container running in CoreOS instance 2. The main disadvantage of this solution is tha it is not possible to provide a virtual tenant network using this solution. This is because all the docker containers are attached to docker0 bridge, which is connected to OVS. OVS acts as a way to provide communication between different server instances.

Attaching container's veth interface to OVS

In this case, all the docker containers in the CoreOS instance are attached directly to the OVS bridge. There will be multiple instance of bridge running inside OVS, each mapping to different customers/tenants. A new bridge needs to be created and provisioned for each tenant in the system. On the subsequent creation of containers (for the same tenant), the container's interface should be connected to the corresponding bridge instance. The OVS bridge provides connectivity to the other CoreOS instances using GRE/VxLAN tunnels.

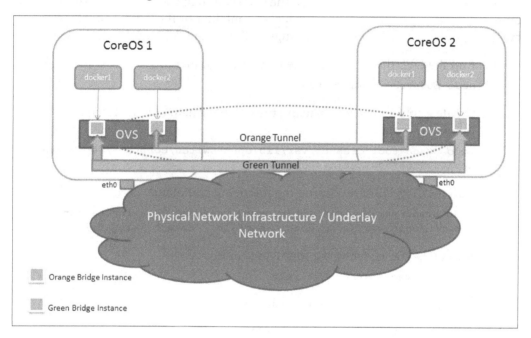

The step-by-step procedure to configure this kind of solution is described in detail as follows. This consists of the following major steps to be performed on both the CoreOS instances:

- Configurations during the instantiation of a CoreOS node in a cluster
- Configurations during the creation of the first container for a tenant
- Configurations during the creation of subsequent containers for a tenant

Configuration in CoreOS Instance 1

This section describes in detail the operations to be performed on the coreos-ovs docker of CoreOS node1 to provide this solution.

Configurations during the instantiation of a CoreOS node in a cluster

During initialization, OVS needs to be started and the procedures to start OVS are as follows. Note that the way in which the OVS command will be executed depends on whether OVS is deployed inside a docker container or the CoreOS host instance. However, in both cases, there is no change in the list of OVS commands to be used.

1. Run the OVS data-path module using the command:

    ```
    sudo modprobe openvswitch
    ```

2. Create a configuration, db, using the default schema file with the following command:

    ```
    sudo ovsdb-tool create /var/lib/openvswitch/conf.db /usr/share/
    openvswitch/vswitch.ovsschema
    ```

3. Run the OVS DB server using the following command:

    ```
    sudo ovsdb-server /var/lib/openvswitch/conf.db --remote=punix:/
    var/run/openvswitch/db.sock --pidfile --detach --log-file
    ```

4. Run OVS-VSCTL using the following command:

    ```
    sudo ovs-vsctl --no-wait init
    ```

5. Run the OVS switchd daemon using the following command:

    ```
    sudo ovs-vswitchd --pidfile --detach
    ```

Configurations during the creation of the first container for a tenant

When a container is created for a tenant for the first time, a new bridge needs to be created and this container should be connected to OVS. The procedure to do this is described in detail as follows:

1. Bring down the docker0 bridge instance (the default bridge created by docker):

    ```
    sudo ip link set dev docker0 down
    ```

2. Detach the virtual interface that is created for the container from docker0 bridge. The virtual interface starts with the name as veth:

```
sudo brctl delif docker0 vethda0657c
```

3. Create a bridge instance for a tenant:

```
sudo ovs-vsctl add-br br0
```

4. Add the port that is created in docker. This interface starts with veth:

```
sudo ovs-vsctl add-port br0 vethda0657c
```

5. Set the IP address of the eth0 interface of the docker container. It is not possible to set the IP address of the docker container inside the docker instance. We need to use the nsenter utility for this. To do this, follow these steps:

   ○ Execute the following command and get the pid:

   ```
   docker inspect --format {{.State.Pid}} <container_name_or_
   ID>
   ```

   ○ Execute the following command and get the pid:

   ```
   sudo nsenter --target $PID --mount --uts --ipc --net --pid
   ifconfig eth0 50.0.0.1
   ```

6. Create a GRE tunnel with the remote node as 172.17.8.103. Here, the assumption is the eth0 IP of CoreOS instance 2 is 172.17.8.103

```
sudo ovs-vsctl add-port br0 gre1 -- set Interface gre1 type=gre
options:remote_ip=172.17.8.103 options:key=100
```

 The key needs to be different for each tunnel.

Configurations during the creation of subsequent containers for a tenant

This section describes the configuration to be done when subsequent containers are being created in the CoreOS instance.

1. Add the port that is created in docker. This interface starts with veth:

```
sudo ovs-vsctl add-port br0 veth640b626
```

2. Create a GRE tunnel with the remote node as 172.17.8.103:

```
sudo ovs-vsctl add-port br0 gre1 -- set Interface gre1 type=gre
options:remote_ip=172.17.8.103 options:key=100
```

Configuration in CoreOS Instance 2

This section describes in detail the operations to be performed on the coreos-ovs docker of CoreOS node2 to provide this solution.

Configurations during the instantiation of a CoreOS node in a cluster

This section describes the list of operations to be performed during the initialization of the CoreOS instance. During initialization, OVS needs to be started and the procedure to start OVS is as follows:

1. Run the OVS data-path module using the command:

   ```
   sudo modprobe openvswitch
   ```

2. Create a configuration, db, using the default schema file with the following command:

   ```
   sudo ovsdb-tool create /var/lib/openvswitch/conf.db /usr/share/
   openvswitch/vswitch.ovsschema
   ```

3. Run the OVS DB server using the following command:

   ```
   sudo ovsdb-server /var/lib/openvswitch/conf.db --remote=punix:/
   var/run/openvswitch/db.sock --pidfile --detach --log-file
   ```

4. Run OVS-VSCTL using the following command:

   ```
   sudo ovs-vsctl --no-wait init
   ```

5. Run the OVS switchd daemon using the following command:

   ```
   sudo ovs-vswitchd --pidfile --detach
   ```

6. Create a bridge instance:

   ```
   sudo ovs-vsctl add-br br0
   ```

7. Create a GRE tunnel with the remote node as `172.17.8.101`. Here, the assumption is the etho IP of CoreOS instance 1 is `172.17.8.101`:

   ```
   sudo ovs-vsctl add-port br0 gre1 -- set Interface gre1 type=gre
   options:remote_ip=172.17.8.101 options:key=100
   ```

 The key needs to be different for each tunnel.

Configurations during the creation of the first container for a tenant

When a container is created for a tenant for the first time, a new bridge needs to be created and this container should be connected to OVS. The procedure to do this is described in detail as follows:

1. Bring down the docker0 bridge instance (the default bridge created by docker):

    ```
    sudo ip link set dev docker0 down
    ```

2. Detach the virtual interface that is created for the container from docker0 bridge. The virtual interface starts with the name as veth:

    ```
    sudo brctl delif docker0 vethda0657c
    ```

3. Create a bridge instance for a tenant:

    ```
    sudo ovs-vsctl add-br br0
    ```

4. Add the port that is created in docker. This interface starts with veth:

    ```
    sudo ovs-vsctl add-port br0 vethda0657c
    ```

5. Set the IP address of the eth0 interface of the docker container. It is not possible to set the IP address of the docker container inside the docker instance. We need to use the `nsenter` utility for this. To do this, follow these steps:

    ○ Execute the following command and get the `pid`:

    ```
    docker inspect --format {{.State.Pid}} <container_name_or_
    ID>
    ```

    ○ Execute the following command and get the `pid`:

    ```
    sudo nsenter --target $PID --mount --uts --ipc --net --pid
    ifconfig eth0 50.0.0.1
    ```

6. Create a GRE tunnel with the remote node as `172.17.8.103`. Here, the assumption is the etho IP of CoreOS instance 2 is `172.17.8.103`:

    ```
    sudo ovs-vsctl add-port br0 gre1 -- set Interface gre1 type=gre
    options:remote_ip=172.17.8.103 options:key=100
    ```

 The key needs to be different for each tunnel.

Configurations during the creation of subsequent containers for a tenant

This section describes the configuration to be done when subsequent containers are being created in the CoreOS instance.

1. Add the port that is created in docker. This interface starts with veth:

    ```
    sudo ovs-vsctl add-port br0 veth640b626
    ```

2. Create a GRE tunnel with the remote node as `172.17.8.103`:

    ```
    sudo ovs-vsctl add-port br0 gre1 -- set Interface gre1 type=gre
    options:remote_ip=172.17.8.103 options:key=100
    ```

Now you should be able to ping from the docker container running in CoreOS instance 1 to a docker container running in CoreOS instance 2. The main advantage of this solution is that it is possible to provide a virtual tenant network using this solution.

Looping issue

Everything works fine so far. However, when the number of CoreOS instances running in the cluster increases, we may need to create a mesh of tunnels between CoreOS instances for each customer/tenant. This ends up creating a loop in the network that will result in a traffic black hole. Let us look into this issue in detail and discuss the solution.

Consider a topology wherein you have three CoreOS instances running in the CoreOS cluster. In each of these instances, the green and orange customers' applications are deployed as a container. To provide VTN for each customer, we need to create tunnels across these CoreOS instances. In this case, we need to create two tunnels for each customer from every CoreOS instance. From CoreOS instance 1, we need to create two tunnels for each customer: one toward CoreOS instance 2 and the other toward CoreOS instance 3. Similarly, from CoreOS instance 2, we need to create two tunnels and so on. This will result in forming a layer2 loop in the customer's bridge instance.

 The total number of tunnels required to create a complete mesh in the topology is 2n-1, where n is the number of CoreOS instances wherein the tenant's service is deployed as a container.

As the bridge instance is a layer2 device, this results in forwarding the same packet multiple times in the loop:

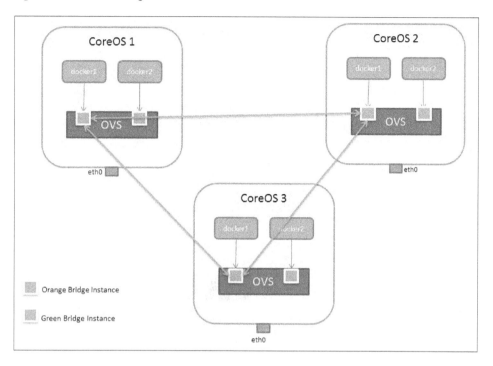

A simple way to avoid this looping problem is by running **Spanning Tree Protocol (STP)** in OVS. STP is defined and standardized as IEEE 802.1D. STP identifies a loop-free topology, considering all the links in the topology based on different metrics. Once it identifies the loop-free topology, it will block one or more ports (in this case, tunnels) that are not part of the loop-free topology. The ports that are in a blocking state won't forward the traffic and hence avoid the traffic black hole.

In the preceding topology, when we run the spanning tree based on the priority or configured bridge-id, STP blocks one port, in this case blocks the port from CoreOS 3 to CoreOS 2:

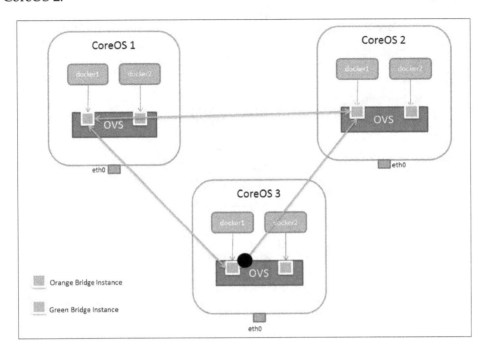

The list of commands to enable and configure the spanning tree in OVS are as follows:

- Enable the spanning tree on a bridge instance:

```
ovs-vsctl set Bridge br0 stp_enable=true
```

- Set the bridge priority:

```
ovs-vsctl set Bridge br0 other_config:stp-priority=0x7800
```

- Set the path cost of the port:

```
ovs-vsctl set Port eth0 other_config:stp-path-cost=10
```

 The bridge priority and path cost configurations are not mandatory configurations.

The spanning tree needs to be enabled on all the bridge instances of OVS to avoid any loop in the network.

Summary

In this chapter, we have seen the importance of OVS in container communications and the various advantages provided by OVS. As there are multiple communication mechanisms available for container communications, while deploying the CoreOS cluster, based on the advantages, ease of use, and network management tools, you should cautiously choose one or more communication mechanisms in your deployment. In the next chapter, we are going to see some of the latest developments in CoreOS and advanced topics such as security, orchestration, container data volume management, and so on.

8
What Next?

In this chapter, we will touch upon some advanced Docker and Core OS topics and we will also discuss what is upcoming in CoreOS. For most of the topics, we will not go into the details of using or deploying each of the features mentioned in this chapter, but will discuss enough so as to be aware of what else is cooking.

This chapter covers the following topics:

- Container security
- Easy upgrade using CoreUpgrade
- User authentication using Dex
- Sysdig
- Other container orchestration mechanisms such as Kubernetes, Apache Mesos, and Swarm
- Docker data volume management
- Open Container Project

Container security

Security is an important aspect of any deployment. There should be security in the applications, devices, and network to disallow any unauthorized access. There should also be security in the container/docker deployment so as to disallow unauthorized access to system resources reserved for the container. We will understand how Docker container ensures network and resource isolation and security.

Docker uses the namespaces to isolate the container from other containers running on the host. There are three important namespaces that take part in providing security:

- **Process namespace**: Each Linux system has a process tree, that is, there is an init process with process ID 1, which is also called the root process. This root process spawns other daemons and processes as a child process. These daemons and processes can then create their own child and so on. It is possible to create a child namespace with one of the child as the root process. All the processes running in the child namespace don't have the knowledge of the parent namespace; hence, they can't perform any operations (like signal) on the processes outside their namespace.

- **Network namespace**: Each container has its own network interface that is different from the host interface's. They have their own loop-back interface as well. The only way containers can talk to the external world is through the bridge network at the host. Bridge network enables communication between different namespaces running in the same host or to an address in another host. This ensures that the network stack is exclusive to the container, thereby running its own IP, TCP, UDP stacks, and so on. Docker has an additional layer of security by allowing communication with another Docker by exposing ports or by creating links to another container explicitly.

- **Resource namespace**: This ensures that each container has its own resource exclusively for its own use. Resource can be dedicated RAM, processors, or a disk with its own filesystem. This ensures that the container usage doesn't cross the set limits, thus ensuring that it doesn't intrude upon the resources being allocated to another container.

The following figure illustrates the isolation provided by the Docker container. As we can see, the service running inside container has its own root process, filesystem, and interface which an operation system would normally provide. These features are present in almost all of the Linux distributions that Docker uses to provide isolation.

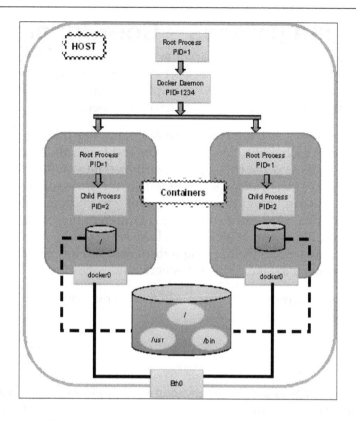

After isolation, let's discuss security. Docker starts container in non-privilege mode. That means containers or applications running inside the container only have permissions to perform actions that don't require root privileges. Some examples are using a port less than 1024 (though non-privileged docker can use ports that are under and above the 1024 range), modifying a file in /etc, mounting a filesystem, and so on. This ensures that even services in containers are hacked; they can't inflict damage on the host and the impact can be limited to that container instance. The allowed privileges can be configured and it can be very restrictive, or very relaxed based on the environment (trusted or non-trusted) containers are expected to work.

Docker also recommends securing the access to Docker Daemon, which runs as root on the host machine. Also, it recommends enabling secure HTTP connections in case it is required to administrate a container remotely. Further, the in-built firewalls in Linux kernel like SELinux can be used to further add restrictions on the Docker to set restrictions for using only specific ports and specific protocols (only TCP, only UDP, and so on). Also, it is advisable to use other Linux security utilities and tools to protect and harden the system.

Update and patches – CoreUpdate

CoreUpdate is a service available as part of `Premium Manged Service` targeted at Enterprise customers who require support and SLA-based support in case they face issues with deployment. CoreUpdate helps to monitor cluster health, cluster software versions, manage updates, and patch deployment.

CoreUpdates provides a web interface and a command-line interface to view the versions running on each of the CoreOS instances and to schedule upgrades on them. All instances of the CoreOS can be logically distributed into multiple application groups, and upgrades can be managed individually for those applications. For instance, they can be configured to pick the upgrade/patch from different channels like stable/beta/alpha. They can be scheduled at different times and can have different metadata, like where to pick the package for upgrade/patch. During the upgrade process, progress of the upgrade is displayed and any error/information/warnings are displayed to take corrective actions.

CoreUpdate also provides a HTTP-based API to integrate software management with the developed application.

Dex

All of us have experienced user authentication in multiple ways, like when we log in to websites, log in to our computer, log in to social sites, and so on. There are a wide variety of authentication systems like local users being managed by a system admin for Linux or Microsoft Windows, Enterprise-wide Active Directory, or LDAP, or through identity providers such as Google, Outlook, Yahoo!, and Facebook.

As an application developer, **Dex** (`https://github.com/coreos/dex`) solves the problem of user authentication by providing a ready-to-use standard-based implementation and connectors for various authentication systems including local authentication. This makes it easier for the developer to concentrate on their business logic and trust that authentication is well taken care of.

Since Dex implementation is based on standard (**OpenID Connect (OIDC) Core spec**), it is language independent as the interfaces are well defined. Use a client library conforming to OIDC corresponding to the programming language and you are good to go.

There are different authentication mechanisms that can be used by integrating off-the-shelf connectors. If we have to draw a parallel, it is very much like a database connector. Currently, two connectors, local and OIDC connector, and more are getting developed. With local connector, the user can log in to the system using the authentication database maintained by Dex locally, like Linux user IDs and passwords. With OIDC connectors, users can be authenticated using another OIDC Identity Provider like Google or another Dex instance as Dex itself is an OIDC identity provider.

So, if you have a requirement for authentication in your system, explore Dex.

sysdig

We are aware of commonly used debugging tools for Linux to monitor and take snapshots of system health. For example, if we want to check whether the machine is overloading its CPU or RAM, we use tools like top or vmstat. If we have to capture the packets over the interface, we use wireshark or tcpdump. Similarly, we use iostat to monitor the system IO devices.

sysdig provides integrated support for monitoring all the preceding system resources along with providing many more features. And most importantly, in our context it provides support for containers. We know that containers run in the host OS in separate namespaces. So the processes running inside containers are also visible to the native tools, say, for example, ps. In a container environment, the information related to the application is present in two levels: one at the host kernel level, for example process ID as the host kernel sees it, and the other at the container level, for example, the process ID inside the container. All native Linux tools give a host kernel view leaving it to the user to correlate information to find out which information pertains to the container and segregate information on a per-container basis. To get information as the container application sees it, Docker interfaces/commands are to be used. sysdig solves this problem.

Let's take a hands-on approach to get a feel of what information sysdig provides.

The first step is to install and run `sysdig`. After we start the docker container for sysdig, we are taken to a shell where we can run the `sysdig` commands.

```
Vagrant ssh core-01
docker pull sysdig/sysdig
docker run -i -t --name sysdig --privileged -v /var/run/docker.sock:/
host/var/run/docker.sock -v /dev:/host/dev -v /proc:/host/proc:ro -v /
boot:/host/boot:ro -v /lib/modules:/host/lib/modules:ro -v /usr:/host/
usr:ro sysdig/sysdig
```

Start a Docker container as daemon using the following command:

```
/usr/bin/docker run –d --name busybox busybox /bin/sh -c "while true; do
echo Hello World; sleep 60; done"
```

We will run some example commands to find out container-specific information. First, we will list the containers running on the machine both using the `docker ps` in another login window and using `sysdig`:

```
docker ps
CONTAINER ID          IMAGE              COMMAND
CREATED               STATUS             PORTS              NAMES
f71277abf37c          busybox            "/bin/sh -c 'while tr"    4
seconds ago           Up 3 seconds                         busybox
d21a39a0668f          sysdig/sysdig      "/docker-entrypoint.s"    5
minutes ago           Up 5 minutes                         sysdig
```

We see here that there are two containers running on the host machine: one container is for `sysdig` and the other is the `busybox` we started. Now, we will run the corresponding `sysdig` command:

```
sysdig -c lscontainers
container.type container.image container.name      container.id
-------------- --------------- ------------------- ------------
docker         busybox         busybox             f74777abf37c
docker         sysdig/sysdig   sysdig              d2da79a0668f
```

The following command shows the cumulative CPU usage of the containers:

```
sysdig -c topcontainers_cpu
```

The output we get is as follows:

Similarly, we can see a list of processes, its corresponding containers, and process ID (as seen by the host and as seen by the container at the global level) by using the following command. Note that the -pc flag indicates that the information is required in the container context. The same command can also be extended by providing a container name, and information is displayed only for that container.

```
sysdig -pc -c topconns
```

The output we get is as follows:

By now, you would have got an idea of the utility of sysdig. Similar to the process and CPU information, it can provide a host of other features like monitoring networks, network IO, disk usage, trace traffic, and so on. And most of the monitoring can be done in a container context also by adding the –pc switch.

Competitive container orchestration mechanism

In this section, we are going to see the other container orchestration mechanism currently available in the market. Some of these orchestration mechanisms can in fact be complementary to the CoreOS orchestration mechanism. As we have already seen in *Chapter 3, Creating Your CoreOS Cluster and Managing the Cluster*, fleet acts as a cluster manager in CoreOS and instantiates the docker units/service in any one of the nodes in the cluster. Let us discuss the other orchestration mechanisms in detail in this chapter. Some of the key container orchestration mechanisms currently available are as follows:

- Kubernetes
- Apache Mesos
- Swarm

Kubernetes

Kubernetes is an open source container orchestration infrastructure developed by Google for deploying containers or a group of containers in a server cluster. Kubernetes provides a way of deploying a group of containers as a single logical service. This group of containers has been termed **pod**. Apart from providing a mechanism for deploying an application or container, Kubernetes also provides way for scheduling, updating, maintaining, and scaling the containers in a cluster.

Kubernetes operates over the pod rather than containers. A pod can contain a single container or a group of logically interrelated containers, as described earlier. Kubernetes consists of the following components:

- Kubernetes master
- Kubernetes nodes (Minion)
- Kubernetes pods
- Kubernetes services

The following diagram illustrates the components of Kubernetes:

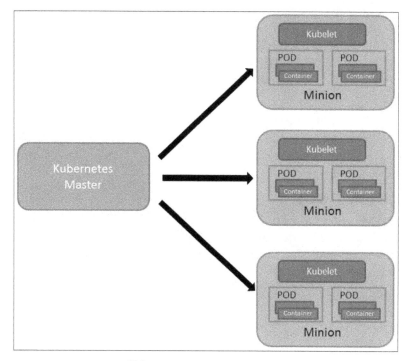

Kubernetes components overview

Kubernetes master

As the name implies, **Kubernetes master** is the master node that controls other nodes and pods in the cluster. It is the control plane and provides the following services:

- Placement of pods in the server
- Replication control of various pods
- Maintaining the state of the containers
- Providing the REST API for controlling the nodes, pods, and so on from the external world

Master Kubernetes runs apiserver, controller manager, and optionally the kubelet and proxy servers.

Kubernetes nodes

Kubernetes nodes are also called the minion. User applications are deployed as a container or docker containers in the minion. The Kubernetes nodes host important services of Kubernetes like kubelet and kube-proxy.

Kubelet is responsible for managing the pods at the node level. It acts as a primary node-agent.

kube-proxy or Kubernetes network proxy is an application that will manage services inside the Kubernetes nodes. This is also responsible for providing a kind of virtual IP for the application running in the nodes.

Kubernetes pods

Kubernetes pods are a group of containers that are logically tightly coupled with each other and running inside the same Kubernetes nodes. The containers that are part of the same pods share resources like storage, networking, and so on. The following represents a pod:

```
apiVersion: v1
kind: Pod
metadata:
  name: backend-app
  labels:
    app: backend-app
    version: v1
    role=backend
spec:
  containers:
  - name: javaapp
    image: kingston/javaapp
    ports:
    - containerPort: 443
    volumeMounts:
    - mountPath: /volumes/logs
      name: logs
  - name: logapp
    image: kingston/logapp:v1.1.3
    ports:
    - containerPort: 9999
    volumeMounts:
    - mountPath: /logs
      name: logs
  - name: monitor
    image: kingston/monitor:v1.5.6
    ports:
    - containerPort: 1234
```

Kubernetes service

Kubernetes service is a group of pods that is running inside the cluster. Services provide the vital features that are required for any kind of pods in the cluster such as load-balancing, application service discovery, easy deployment, and so on. A service is described in JSON representation as follows:

```json
{
    "kind": "Service",
    "apiVersion": "v1",
    "metadata": {
        "name": "Web Frontend Service"
    },
    "spec": {
        "selector": {
            "app": "webapp",
            "role": "frontend"
        },
        "ports": [
            {
                "name": "http"
                "protocol": "TCP",
                "port": 80,
                "targetPort": 80
            }
        ]
    }
}
```

Now, we have seen the basics of Kubernetes. Let us look into how Kubernetes can be used as an orchestration framework for CoreOS docker/Rackt containers.

CoreOS and Kubernetes

Kubernetes can also be used to provide advanced cluster-wide orchestration in CoreOS using an etcd distributed key-value store. As Kubernetes is a powerful tool for container orchestration, which provides the essential features of a typical deployment such as automatic load-balancing, service discovery, and container replication, in a CoreOS environment, Kubernetes can be used as a container orchestration framework.

One node inside the CoreOS cluster can act as a Kubernetes master, wherein you can run the apiserver and controller manager. All other nodes in the CoreOS cluster can act as a minion, wherein you can install and run kubelet and kube-proxy.

Kubernetes can also be used to provide advanced cluster-wide orchestration in CoreOS using an etcd distributed key-value store.

Apache-Mesos

Apache-Mesos is a container cluster manager developed for very large clusters involving thousands of hosts. Mesos provides a distributed kernel that is running across different nodes in the cluster and provides APIs for the application to manage resources such as memory, CPU, disk, and scheduling these resources.

The major components of Mesos are as follows:

- Mesos agent
- Mesos master
- ZooKeeper
- Mesos frameworks

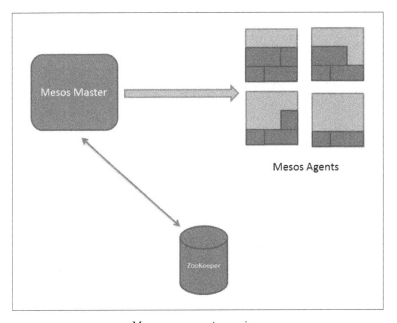

Mesos component overview

Mesos master

The **Mesos master** daemon runs in the master node that manages all the slave nodes or agents and the Mesos frameworks. The master takes care of sharing the resource to the frameworks based on the configured scheduling policy, which can either be strict priority or fair sharing.

Mesos agent

Mesos agent is responsible for running the actual tasks. The agent reports to the master about the availability of the resources, which the master agent uses to allocate a particular task or framework to be ran on the agent.

ZooKeeper

In a typical Mesos deployment, there will be more than one master available to avoid single point of failure. In these cases, **ZooKeeper** is used to elect the leader among the available masters.

Mesos frameworks

Mesos frameworks are the ones that run the tasks in the Mesos agent. The framework consists of two components: a scheduler that registers with the master and an executor that executes the tasks in the slave node. The master determines the number of resources to be allocated for the framework and allocates it to the framework. The scheduler picks the resource offered from this list.

Swarm

Swarm is a native orchestration mechanism provided by Docker. Like other orchestration mechanisms, Swarm also consists of Swarm master and Swarm agent.

Swarm master takes care of orchestrating the docker container to different Swarm agents. The master will be running in one or two nodes in the cluster whereas the **Swarm agent** will be running in all the nodes in the network.

Docker data volume management

One of the main aspects of the container that we haven't discussed until now is the container's data volume management. In this section, we are going to see some basic concepts of container data volume management, some of the major problems in data volume management, and their solutions.

As you may be aware, the docker container provides two different ways of managing the data volumes as:

- Data volumes
- Data volume containers

The preceding two mechanisms provide various ways for storing the data in a persistent volume, a way to mount a host directory as a data volume, a way to mount a host file as a data volume, and so on. This works well until the containers are tied to a particular node/server in the cluster.

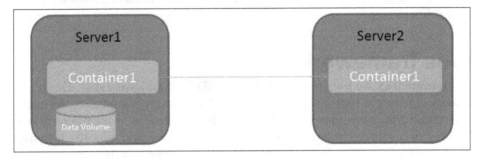

Docker data volume management

When the container is moving from one server to another server, the data volume should also be moved. Typically, the data volume won't be moved when the container is moved from one node to another. This is because the docker/orchestration layer manages the containers and data volume separately.

Here comes the necessity of managing these two entities together. Flocker provides a way of managing both the docker container and docker volume together.

Flocker can be used along with container orchestration mechanisms such as Kubernetes and Mesos. Work has been going on to integrate Flocker with CoreOS, though some non-production-ready deployments are already available with CoreOS.

Introduction to Flocker

Flocker is an open source container data volume manager to manage data volumes. In docker, a data volume is tied to a single server. However, in Flocker, the data volume, which is also called a dataset, is portable and hence can be used with any server in the cluster. Flocker manages the docker container along with the data volumes. Hence, when a container is moved from one server to another server in the cluster, the corresponding data volume will also be moved.

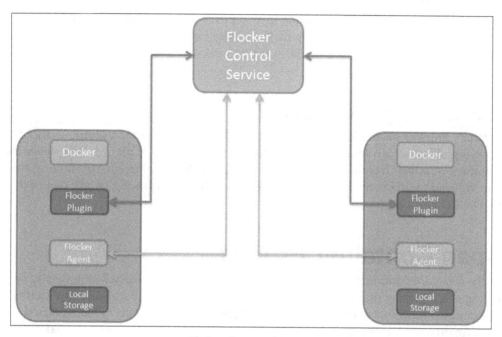

Flocker cluster architecture

The Flocker cluster architecture consists of the following components/services:

- Flocker control services
- Flocker agents
- Flocker plugin for Docker

Flocker control services

In Kubernetes, we have Kubernetes master, and similarly the **Flocker control service** acts as a master and is installed on a single node in the cluster. It exposes the REST API to interface with an external application. This is the brain of Flocker and enables the user to monitor the state of the cluster.

Flocker agents

Flocker agents receive the commands from control services and make sure that the state of the Flocker agent matches with the desired state. When the local state is not matching the desired state, it calculates the actions necessary to make the local state match the desired configuration.

Flocker plugin for Docker

Docker's Flocker plugin deploys a container along with the data volume without worrying about which server in the cluster the data volume is placed. Whenever the container is moved from one server to another, the plugin takes care of moving the data volume too. This makes sure that the data volume is running in any one node in the Flocker cluster.

Open Container Project

As the different container technologies are being developed, there is a necessity of having a standard container format in order to provide interoperability and define the standard for the containers. In order to achieve this, the CoreOS team started working on a container standardization mechanism called *App Container* to define the standard container image format, runtime environment, and discovery protocol, to work toward the goal of a standard, portable shipping container for applications.

Meanwhile, the **Open Container Project (OCP)** was formed by a large group of industry leaders to define the standard. The Open Container Project is hosted under Linux Foundation. CoreOS App Container also contributes to OCP and the latest specification of the OCP project can be found at the following link: `https://github.com/opencontainers/specs`

Summary

As CoreOS is a young and very promising operating system, a lot of developments are happening on daily basis. One of the major milestones of CoreOS in the recent past was that Google and CoreOS jointly announced a new project called Tectonic to offer IT infrastructure, which is completely container-based leveraging both CoreOS and Kubernetes. Tectonic is a commercial Kubernetes platform that combines the CoreOS stack with Kubernetes to bring a Google-style infrastructure to any cloud. Companies such as Rackspace, Salesforce, MemSQL, Atlassian, and Pivotal's Cloud Foundry have already deployed CoreOS. The future of CoreOS looks very bright as CoreOS is aiming to build next-generation IT infrastructure without increasing the complexity. As security is one of the major concerns in current IT infrastructure, one of the major goals of CoreOS is to enable the companies to run their applications securely and reliably in any environment, bringing a promising future for CoreOS.

Index